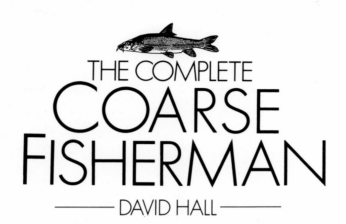

THE COMPLETE
COARSE
FISHERMAN

— DAVID HALL —

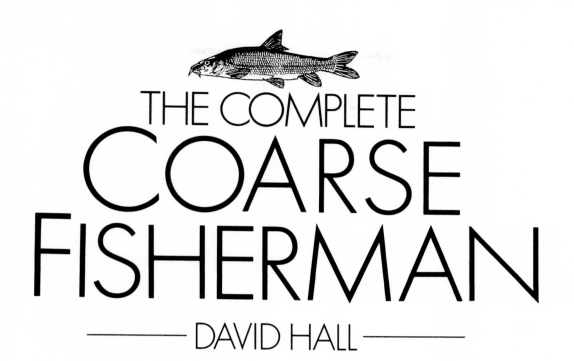

THE COMPLETE
COARSE
FISHERMAN

—— DAVID HALL ——

Ward Lock Limited · London

First published in Great Britain 1980
by Ward Lock Limited,
8 Clifford Street,
London W1X 1RB, an Egmont Company.

Reprinted 1982
New edition 1987

This edition produced for Ward Lock Limited by
Curtis Garratt Limited, The Old Vicarage,
Horton-cum-Studley, Oxford OX9 IBT
Layout by Jerry Burman
Diagrams by Taurus Graphics
Index by Barbara James
Text filmset by Lightning Graphics

Printed in Portugal by Resopal

British Library Cataloguing in Publication Data

Hall, David
   The complete coarse fisherman.
   1. Fishing
   I. Title
   799.1'2   SH439

ISBN 0–7063–6554–2

CONTENTS

INTRODUCTION

Like so many anglers, my introduction to the world of coarse fishing came when I was a youngster on a local pond near my parents' home in Manchester. My tackle consisted of a 3 ft (1 m) garden cane and a length of cotton; a matchstick was my first float and I caught sticklebacks, hundreds of them. The great joy of fishing is that anyone can do it; it doesn't require any special talent or a good sense of timing, like football or cricket. All that is needed is the desire to catch fish, practice and, if you are to be successful, dedication.

The contents of *The Complete Coarse Fisherman* are the results of my dedication. I don't pretend to know all the answers, nobody does, but I have been fortunate enough to make friends, and fish with some of the best anglers in the country, such as Ivan Marks, Richard Walker, Ken Giles and Peter Stone, all of whom have contributed to my knowledge of coarse fishing.

One of the delights of fishing is that having mastered the basics, the extent of one's involvement is purely personal. The angler fishing a local lake once a week or once a month can derive as much satisfaction from the sport as the top match angler winning a big match or a specimen hunter catching a 30 lb (13.50 kg) carp. It is a most singular sport; in fact, I can think of no other sport where the man alone can derive such pleasure. There are no boundaries in coarse fishing and few rules to worry about.

A net of chub from the Warwickshire Avon at Evesham.

For some years now, I have been domiciled in the Midlands and whilst I am not lucky enough to live by a river, I have easy access to many: the River Welland, the Nene and the Ouse in the East; the Avon, the Wye and the Severn in the West and the Trent only forty minutes away, thanks to the constructors of the M1 motorway - a wealth of fishing. Unlike the angler born and bred on a river, my travels have exposed me to all types of fishing: the stick float on the Trent; the swingtip on the Fenland drains; the waggler on the Avon; the swimfeeder on the Severn and the big balsa float on the Wye; methods conceived by top anglers to produce the best results.

There is much to be said for being the master of your river. Many anglers achieve this objective, and none more so than the Nottingham anglers, Frank Barlow, Johnny Rolfe, Pete Palmer and Wayne Swinscoe - great Trent anglers. I love the Trent; it holds such a good head of fish, but I love variety: bream fishing in the Fens during the high summer; barbel fishing on the Severn in late autumn and then on to the Trent in the winter for the roach and the chub fishing. In between all of that, fishing the many lakes and gravel pits that abound in my area, Coombe Abbey lakes, Thrapston gravel pits, Napton, Daventry and Boddington reservoirs.

It is the knowledge gained from fishing these waters that is contained in this book: the baits I use; my approach to the waters I fish; the methods I use. I assume nothing, other than the fact that, by purchasing this book, you seek to become a better angler.

Fishing is changing all the time. The swimfeeder has been a tremendous innovation in recent years. During the mid-seventies, we saw it develop from a crude 'chuck it and chance it' method to a feared tool in the hands of the thinking angler. The springtip, originally conceived by Harold Pattison and later developed into the variable spring and quivertip by Leicester's Trevor ('Brains') Tomlin, has almost made the traditional swingtip obsolete. Carbon fibre rods, many weighing only 5-6 oz (140-170 g) and costing upwards of £100, are now commonplace, whilst monofilament line is available in gossamer thickness.

Change is taking place constantly, but the basics remain the same; casting, feeding, understanding fish behaviour, these things never change. A well-presented bait, using the crudest of tackle will always produce more fish than a poorly presented bait, regardless of the angler's tackle. The angler who can cast accurately and feed his swim properly is halfway to becoming the complete coarse fisherman. Good tackle is important, but it does not automatically make the owner a better angler. If an angler fishes incorrectly with bad tackle, the acquisition of more expensive tackle will not resolve the problem.

The great angler, Ken Giles once said, 'You get out of fishing what you put in', and I believe that to be true. I have put all I know into this book and I hope that you derive as much pleasure from reading it as I did from writing it.

1
CHOOSING THE RIGHT TACKLE

If you are to become a successful angler - and by that, I mean an angler who catches fish consistently on different venues, in differing conditions - it is crucial that you develop a total undertstanding of your tackle set-up. It is not necessary to own the most up-to-date carbon fibre rod or the very latest fast-retrieve fixed-spool reel in order to be successful. What is important is that your tackle is used with the maximum amount of efficiency.

Rods

Since the advent of glass fibre some years ago, the construction of fishing rods has become much more sophisticated; so much so, that very few poor rods are made these days. There are exceptions of course, the 6 ft (1.85 m) solid glass rods which some shops sell as 'boys' rods' are bad investments; they hamper the young angler's progress. If you have a young child, or you are a youngster yourself, who would like to take up the sport, then start off with a 10-13 ft (3-4 m) pole or a 10 ft (3.05 m) rod. Once the young angler has grown to an age or size when he can graduate to a 12-13 ft (3.65-3.95 m) rod, which is the ideal size, the pole or the 10 ft (3.05 m) rod will remain a useful part of his equipment.

In order to be a successful float angler, you must own one or more float rods; these can be 12, 13 or 14 ft (3.65, 3.95 or 4.25 m) in length, depending on your height and preference.. Being only 5 ft 9 in (1.75 m) tall, I use 12 ft (3.65 m) rods. Taller men sometimes prefer longer rods, but quite honestly, it doesn't make too

much difference, although it is an acknowledged fact that whilst most manufacturers are successful in designing and building good actioned 12 ft (3.65 m) rods, very few have been as successful with the longer 13 and 14 ft (3.95 m and 4.25 m) rods. Having equipped yourself with a float rod, which you are satisfied suits you, you must now come to terms with it. I know that Ivan Marks fishes with very fine lines. Most match anglers do and their rods are designed in such a way as to make this possible. Yours might not be, so spend some time getting to know what the rod will do, and make sure that it will suit your specific requirements.

Because of the tremendous amount of information that is published in the angling press each week, it is very easy for the newcomer to get a false impression of angling. Some years ago a youngster wrote to me asking why Ivan Marks could catch fish on the River Welland using a size 20 hook and 1 lb (0.45 kg) line, and yet every time the youngster cast his ½ oz (15 g) bomb across the Welland, his line broke. Apparently he had seen a headline in one of the angling weeklies which stated, 'Ivan Marks lands 30 lb of bream on size 20 hook and 1lb line', so he decided to try this method himself. What the youngster had not realized was that Ivan was using a 3 lb (1.35 kg) reel line; only the hook length was of a 1 lb (0.45 kg) breaking strain, and his bomb was tied to much stronger line. Top match anglers do use fine tackle, but their rods are designed for that pur-

Overleaf: *Nobby Clark landing a 3.5-lb (1.5-kg) chub from a snaggy swim.*

pose, while the average float rod selling at £10-20 is not. Furthermore, unless you find yourself fishing against top-flight anglers, it is not necessary to emulate them.

Lines

The top match angler is constantly striving to improve his bait presentation, because he is confronted with having to catch the maximum amount of fish in the minimum amount of time from a very small area of water. The pleasure angler has no such restrictions, so the need to fish with tiny hooks and ultrafine lines does not apply to the same extent. However, it is worth remembering that because a finer line will allow a bait to fall more naturally through the water, more bites will be encountered by the angler who fishes with a 2 lb (0.90 kg) line than, say, an angler fishing with a 5 lb (2.25 kg) line. As a rule of thumb, I would suggest that a 2.5 lb (1.10 kg) reel line with a 1.7 lb (0.77 kg) or 2 lb (0.90 kg) hook length will suffice under most circumstances, but if you happen to be fishing a swim which houses a snag or you are fishing for big fish, then commonsense suggests you use a heavier line. I never use any line heavier than 5 lb (2.25 kg), but I know a number of very successful specimen hunters who very often use 8, 9 and 10 lb (3.50, 4 and 4.50 kg) line.

Your choice of line is important: cheap line is false economy, so always buy quality line. The difference in price between a poor line and a high-quality one is possibly only a matter of a few pence, but the quality line will last you up to six months, depending on how much fishing you do, and will account for many good fish. The cheaper one will show signs of wear very quickly and will invariably cost you a good fish. Something many anglers do not realize is that similar lines often behave differently from one another. Some lines sink and these are ideal for waggler fishing or legering. Personally I use Maxima, for all my waggler and leger fishing and either Racine Tortue or Beyer Perlon for stick float fishing. Of course, these are my preferences and you may find something which is more suitable to your style of fishing.

A modern glass fibre match rod. Note the fine tip which makes the rod suitable for use with fine lines.

While on the subject of monofilament lines, there have been a number of pre-stretched lines on the market for some time now. It is suggested by the manufacturers that this type of line is stronger than ordinary line, but I have never been particularly confident fishing with it, as I feel that the elasticity in normal non-stretched lines acts as a buffer if I have to strike hard in order to set the hook home when fishing at a distance.

Reels

It is an acknowledged fact that the British anglers are the finest exponents of rod and reel fishing in the world, and yet until recent years, very few fixed-spool reels were made for the British market. Most of the major manufacturers produced spinning reels for the large American and European markets. Some modified these reels to make them more suitable for the British market, whilst others, mainly Japanese companies, were content to sell reels which were not really suited to British styles of fishing. Nevertheless, they were inexpensive to purchase.

Choosing a reel is important. Some anglers purchase a different reel for different jobs; others perhaps only own one, which is used for float fishing and legering. Your choice of reel is just as important as your choice of a rod, and whilst finance is always a major consideration, it does pay to buy the best reel you can afford. The chances are that if you buy wisely your reel will last for ten or more years. Since it was intro-

duced in 1969, the Mitchell Match fixed-spool reel has been the first choice for many anglers, as it offers the unique facility of an automatic bale arm.

The American and Japanese manufacturers are now producing reels designed for the British market, many with the increasingly popular skirted spool, a feature which is designed to eliminate the problem of line gathering behind the spool. There is also a number of closed-face reels on the market, ABU being the most successful with their 500 series. I have owned a number of closed-face reels. I think it would be fair to say that when they are working properly, they are the best reels in the world, but sadly, I have never owned one that has worked well

Always fill your spool with line to capacity.

consistently; perhaps I have just been unlucky.

When you buy your first reel, be it for a child, a friend or for yourself, try to think ahead. A Mitchell 410 or a quality Japanese reel will still be a useful reel to own in a few year's time when you or your child have graduated to more sophisticated tackle.

It is of prime importance to fill the spool correctly; I still see anglers fishing with half empty spools, and yet in order to cast efficiently, a spool must be filled to capacity. I can think of no other sport where the participants handicap themselves to quite the same extent as anglers. Can you imagine footballers putting their boots on the wrong feet, or an athlete choosing to run in heavy boots? If you are to be successful you have to take advantage of every opportunity; a spool that is not fully filled can restrict your casting ability by as much as 70 per cent. Think of it this way: you have a rod costing perhaps £25, and a reel costing approximately the same, yet you cannot cast 33 yd (30 m) to the fish because you did not spend an extra 80p on the 110 yd (100 m) of line to fill your spool.

A good-quality, open-faced, fixed-spool reel.

A fixed-spool reel with a closed face.

Hooks

Hooks tend to be a personal thing. For float fishing I favour barbless hooks for two reasons: firstly I feel that they penetrate better and secondly - this applies particularly to the smaller sizes - it is easier to unhook the fish.

Among my angling colleagues, there seems to be a trend towards using barbless hooks. This may be influenced by the fact that more patterns are now available than have been in the past. For legering, particularly when the bait is worm or double maggot , I tend to use the traditional barbed hook. I do this simply because I find that a worm, which tends to be presented stationary for long periods, can wriggle off a barbless hook, whereas the barb will keep it on. I learned that lesson the hard way.

The choice of hook is largely a question of confidence. Most match anglers are quite happy to fish with tiny hooks, arguing that the smaller the hook the more bites they will get, even if they do lose a few fish. The specimen hunter, on the other hand, uses large hooks, arguing that when he gets a bite, he wants to be sure that the fish is well and truly hooked. It should be the bait that dictates the size of the hook that you use. Obviously a fish hooked on a large hook is less likely to be lost than one on a tiny fine wire hook, but whenever we fish or

Opposite: A 5-lb (2.2-kg) tench taken from a Norfolk lake on a good Avon-type rod.

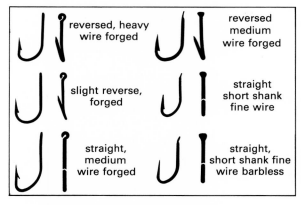

A selection of eyed and spade-end hooks.

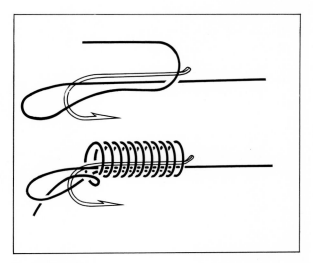

Tying spade-end hooks.

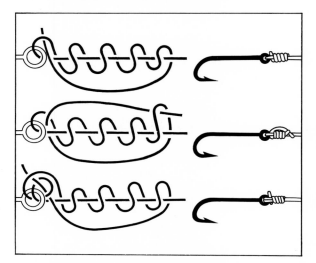

Ways of tying eyed hooks, and swivels.

for whatever species we fish, bait presentation is the key. There are certain baits which will allow us to use a big hook, bread being a prime example. It is quite easy to bury a size 4 hook into a thumbnail-sized piece of flake. Conversely, a single maggot presented on such a hook would look more than a little suspicious. For general fishing I would use either a size 16 hook or a size 18, the size 16 for double maggot and the size 18 for a single maggot.

Balanced tackle

Because no single item is responsible for the capture of fish on its own, it is essential that we fish with balanced tackle, and by that I mean, each single item of tackle should complement

the others. It is pointless using 5 lb (2.25 kg) line in conjunction with a fine tip-actioned match rod. Conversely, it would be equally pointless to use 2 lb (0.90 kg) line in conjunction with a carp rod.   We first have to establish what we are fishing for. If your preference is for big fish, such as carp, barbel, pike and so on, then the tackle has to be robust. A 10 or 11 ft (3.05 or 3.35 m) carp rod with a 2 lb (0.90 kg) test curve will serve most purposes. It can be used in conjunction with lines ranging from 4-10 lb (1.80-4.50 kg). If, on the other hand, your preference is for general fishing - roach, bream, chub, perch - then a 12 ft (3.65 m) float road or match rod will be sufficient. But remember that the majority of these rods are designed for use with lines of 2-4 lb (0.90-1.80 kg) breaking strain with 4 lb (1.80 kg) often being the optimum. If you use heavier lines with these rods and you hook a big fish, there is a chance that in the hands of an inexperienced angler the rod will break before the line.

The key to success is confidence, both in your own ability and your tackle. As I have already stated, tackle does not catch fish, but badly chosen tackle can prevent you from catching, so understand your tackle; ensure that it is balanced properly; then, and only then, can you start to think about becoming the complete coarse fisherman.

2
FISH BEHAVIOUR

Before we can start to catch good bags of fish consistently, we have to try to understand fish behaviour; this is often described in books or magazines as 'watercraft'. What that means, quite simply, is learning to understand fish: why they reside in certain areas of a lake or pond; why they will accept a certain type of bait in the summer, but not in the winter; and why they will accept a moving bait one day but then refuse it the next.

It is accepted that 10 per cent of all anglers catch 90 per cent of the fish; the reasons for this are numerous. Thousands of anglers fish merely for pleasure, and if they catch a few fish, that is a bonus. You can see this type of angler every weekend at your local gravel pit. Invariably they are the ones fishing nearest the car park; not for them the long walk to the better

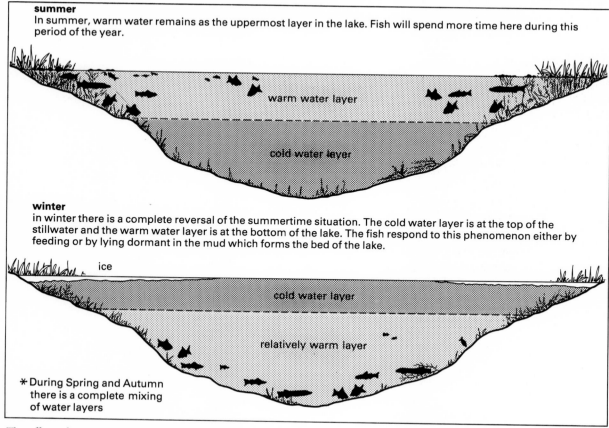

summer
In summer, warm water remains as the uppermost layer in the lake. Fish will spend more time here during this period of the year.

warm water layer

cold water layer

winter
in winter there is a complete reversal of the summertime situation. The cold water layer is at the top of the stillwater and the warm water layer is at the bottom of the lake. The fish respond to this phenomenon either by feeding or by lying dormant in the mud which forms the bed of the lake.

ice

cold water layer

relatively warm layer

✱ During Spring and Autumn there is a complete mixing of water layers

The effect of water temperature on fish behaviour.

David Ball fishing for tench on a large, wind-blown gravel pit.

pegs, they are content to relax, take in the fresh air and hopefully catch a fish or two. Do not misunderstand me for I am not criticizing these anglers. Angling is a sport and you get out of it what you want, and if anglers are content with what they are catching, then the object of the exercise is achieved.

No other sport is affected by the elements quite to the same degree as angling; a sharp overnight frost will make it difficult for even the best anglers to catch fish. Similarly a heavy downpour can turn a normally easy paced river, like the Nene, into a raging torrent and the chance of a good bag of fish becomes very remote. But by learning to understand how fish react to the changing conditions we can increase our chances of catching.

Stillwaters

Many anglers assume that fish residing in a lake or a pond simply swim round and round. This, of course, is not true. It has been proved that with the exception of those occasions when fish migrate from one part of the water to another, as they do from the deeper water in the spring, into the shallower water where they spend the summer months, they seldom move very far at all. They certainly never swim around in circles.

A fish is motivated by three factors: the need to eat, the need to spawn and the need to stay alive. Pike, zander and perch are far greater threats to roach and bream than anglers. Accepting that fish do not swim around in circles, but are prepared to feed, then the first question we must ask ourselves when we approach a water for the first time is, where are the fish likely to be living? The answer is, where the food is.

Let me now dispel a long-standing theory: there is no such thing as a stillwater fishery, all waters move whether they be in a lake, a pond or a reservoir. It is crucial that this fact is acknowledged if you are to be successful. This movement is created by the wind, which causes surface movement. However, once the moving water reaches the bank towards which it is

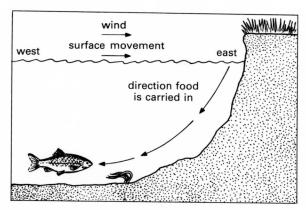

The surface tow is opposite to the current.

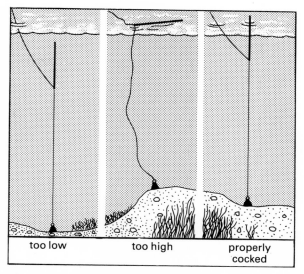

Plumbing the depth of your swim is important if the float is to be properly cocked.

being blown, it is turned under and the bottom layer of water begins to move in the opposite direction. So, assuming that the wind is blowing from west to east, we have a situation whereby the surface water, i.e., the top 12 in (30 cm) is also moving in that direction, whilst the water underneath is moving from east to west.

It is often stated by angling writers that to get the best results, anglers should always fish into the wind. This theory is partly correct, in the respect that the water movement will cause the natural food, i.e., algae, to be moved towards the bank on to which the wind is blowing. I say partly correct, because once again we are led to believe that fish move quite considerable distances in search of food. The prevailing wind in the United Kingdom is westerly and on most stillwaters, particularly in the summer and autumn, when fish are at their most active, a large proportion of the fish population will be found living on the east side of the water. I can think of dozens of waters where this phenomenon exists. Of course there are exceptions, but as a general rule, assuming that the water on this bank isn't too deep or silted up, I would tend to show a preference for this area were I visiting the water for the first time.

Fish behaviour on stillwaters is often governed by the depth of the water. Invariably the fish will tend to inhabit the shallower areas in the summer and the deeper water in the winter. The reason for this is that the shallow water tends to support an abundance of plant life during the summer months, offering both food and cover for the fish, whilst the deeper water tends to be slightly warmer in the winter. Bearing this in mind, it is not difficult to understand why a spot which has produced several good bags of fish in the summer can prove fruitless in the winter: the fish have moved.

But let us go back to water movement on stillwaters. Anybody who has observed fish in moving waters will have noted that they always face upstream; they do this because they can observe and intercept food being carried downstream towards them. With this in mind it follows that wherever there is water movement, fish will face towards the flow. Of all the anglers I see fishing on stillwaters 90 per cent allow their float to drift with the surface pull, which is the opposite way to their loose fed samples which have fallen naturally through the water and are now drifting towards the fish. We strive constantly to present our bait as naturally as possible to the fish, but there is nothing natural about a bait which is travelling in the opposite direction to the current. On stillwaters, try to use a float which is long enough to get beneath the surface drift, this will stop your float from drifting and you will be able to present your bait in a natural manner.

Plumbing the depth of the river or lake you are about to fish is a job that nobody enjoys, but it is crucial, not just because it tells you the

A view of Topcliffe weir pool; this is a favourite haunt of chub and barbel. The anglers are fishing in the highly oxygenated water close to the weir itself.

depth of the water, but more importantly, it can show you where the shelves are. The bottom of a shelf is a prime holding area for fish because food is deposited there by water movement and as I said earlier, the fish are where the food is.

Rivers

Fish in rivers tend to behave differently from stillwater fish, principally because they are exposed to a different set of conditions. In fact, a species of fish in one river will behave in a totally different manner from the same species in another water, and this factor must always be taken into consideration. The seasons of the year also seem to be more in evidence in rivers than in stillwaters. It is quite possible to fish on a stillwater in June and catch good bags of roach, whereas roach in rivers seldom seem to feed with any enthusiasm until the autumn: why this would be I do know. Many pleasure anglers avoid fishing rivers, because they are more demanding than stillwaters, and yet once mastered, rivers will invariably produce a much greater variety of fishing and result in the angler developing a greater knowledge of the sport. The angler who restricts his fishing to stillwaters can develop a thorough knowledge of the behaviour of the fish which live therein, and he

Big-fish angler, Steve Harper, poses with a super 11 lb 14 oz (5.3-kg) barbel from the fast-flowing River Wensum.

can become adept at catching them, but he is limited to catching only those fish which reside in stillwaters. He will have little opportunity of fishing for two of the most exciting fish that live in our rivers, chub and barbel.

Chub and barbel are river fish. Although both have been introduced into stillwaters, there is little indication of them spawning successfully; they are more at home in rivers. Both of these species offer the angler a real challenge, the barbel for its size and tremendous fighting qualities, the chub for its love of snags. Chub is a shoaling fish which responds to most of the acknowledged baits, and offers wonderful sport during the autumn months.

Summer is the time for catching bream and barbel on our rivers and yet the type of water they choose to inhabit could not be more different. For barbel, it is fast shallow water, as found on the Severn or the Hampshire Avon. Bream, on the other hand, prefer the slower deeper waters of East Anglia, in rivers like the Welland and the Nene. There are exceptions of course; for example, there are both bream and barbel in the River Trent. Come the autumn, chub and roach start to respond more readily to anglers' baits, continuing to feed right through the winter until early spring.

Currents play a major part in our understanding of fish behaviour in rivers. Food is carried

An angler cradles a 3-lb (1.3-kg) chub. Find a snag and you are sure to find a chub.

along on the current and deposited in the steady water on the inside of bends, always a good holding area for fish. Most fish will seek the sanctuary of the steady water, found close to the bank on our faster-flowing rivers, such as the Trent, Ribble and Derwent. Few fish are caught in the fast-flowing water; the closer to the bank we fish the steadier the water. Like stillwaters, rivers have shelves and undulations where food is trapped and it holds the fish.

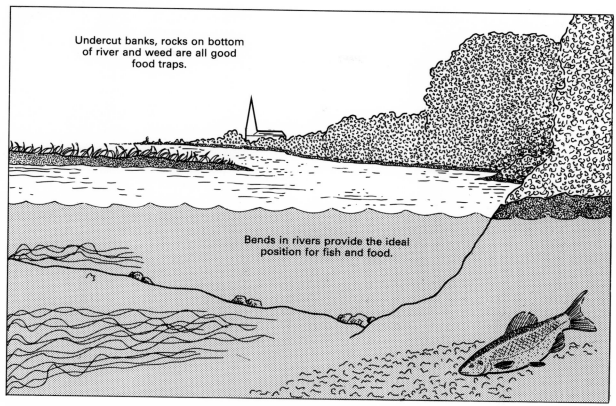

The course of a river and the positions of food in relation to fish behaviour.

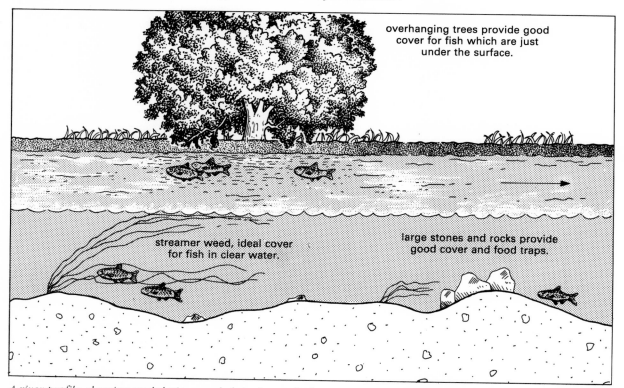

A river profile, showing undulations and obstacles on the bottom as well as overhanging trees in relation to fish.

Graham Marsden returns a bream from a noted Shannon hot spot. Fish live in this area throughout the summer but, with the onset of winter, the river rises and begins to flow, and the fish then move into the backwaters.

Obstacles in the river are also good holding areas for fish; a fallen tree or an overhanging willow will often house a shoal of hungry chub.

Some years ago Ivan Marks wrote an article entitled 'Fishing for Bites'. The point that piece made was simply that the angler who sets out just to catch fish is liable to fish in the most convenient spot, his reasoning being that he is as likely to catch a fish there as anywhere else. On the other hand, the angler who sets out to fish for bites has to think about his fishing; where is he most likely to get his bites?

The angler who thinks about fish behaviour

will invariably catch more fish than the man who does not, in the same way that the angler fishing with balanced tackle will be more successful than the angler who tries to fish with a carp rod and 2 lb (0.90 kg) line. Unlike in other sports our quarry is unseen and it is easy to make excuses for our lack of success: it was too sunny, it was too cold, and so on. Of course, all anglers, even the very best, have bad days but they should be few and far between. Try to fish where you think the fish will be; try to understand fish behaviour and I guarantee you will catch more fish.

3
THE COARSE FISH

Barbel *Barbus barbus*

Found mainly in fast streamy rivers, like the Hampshire Avon, the Dorset Stour, the Severn, and latterly the Trent and its tributaries, the barbel is, for its weight, one of the hardest-fighting species.

Often growing in excess of 10 lb (4.50 kg), the torpedo shape of the barbel and its ability to hug the bottom make it a very sporting fish. With its underslung mouth, it is very much a bottom feeder, and it will take all manner of different baits; maggots, casters, luncheon meat, hemp, bread and worms have all accounted for this species.

Until about fifteen years ago the Hampshire Avon and the Dorset Stour were the rivers normally associated with this species, but since their introduction into the River Severn in the mid-1960s, they have spread and multiplied to such a degree that they can now be caught almost throughout the river. Certainly, fish have been taken as far downstream as Tewkesbury, with catches even in matches exceeding 100 lb (450 kg) during the summer months.

Although barbel can be caught by most known methods, in recent years the swimfeeder/maggot combination has proved to be the most effective, especially on the Severn and the Trent. The use of maggots is barred during

the summer months on a number of stretches of the Stour and Hampshire Avon, so the traditional methods of legered luncheon meat, hemp, bread and worms are practised most on these venues.

It is possible to catch a fish without putting in any feed at all, other than that which is on the hook, but that is merely to 'chuck it and chance it', unless of course you are casting to a particular fish. Because the angler is limited to the amount of time which he can spend at the water's edge, it is not unreasonable that he should want to catch as many fish as possible whilst he is there. The problem is, how do you concentrate your feed into a small area on a river that is running hard? The answer is, by using the blockend swimfeeder.

Prior to the summer of 1975 it was not unusual to hear of matches being won on the Severn with 35 lb (15.80 kg) of chub and barbel; this weight would invariably have been taken on the float. But in 1975 the match anglers discovered the swimfeeder and immediately weights rocketed, with as many as twenty anglers catching in excess of 60 lb (27.20 kg) of barbel in a single match. Quite simply, a large blockend feeder filled to capacity was cast into the fast streamy waters. Provided that it was cast to roughly the same spot each time, a steady build-up of feed began to emerge, as each cast deposited more maggots in the swim. Barbel are very much shoaling fish, especially in the 2-4 lb (900 g-1.8 kg) bracket; therefore loose-fed maggots, which were used previously, would be carried downstream by the flow, spreading the shoal. The opposite hap-

Barbel.

pened with the feeder; the maggots were deposited in a small area on the bottom, and consequently the shoal was kept very tight.

As with all aspects of fishing, the method of catching barbel on the feeder has undergone a tremendous development since its conception in the mid-1970s. No longer are anglers fishing with carp rods, 10 lb (4.50 kg) line and size 8 hooks, although I suspect that fish could still be caught by that method. Nowadays, an Avon rod or one of the now-popular Feeder rods is the order of the day. The Peter Drennan Feeder-links have replaced the massive blockend feeders and 5 lb or 6 lb (2.25 or 2.70 kg) line tied direct to a size 16 or 18 hook is preferred.

Barbel are very much summer fish, although they can be caught throughout the year. However, as the year wears on and the first frosts of winter send the water temperature down, the massive bags which can be expected in July and August begin to diminish. Because of their preference for fast water, barbel are used to taking food at speed. In fact, barbel tend to intercept a bait then turn with it; this accounts for their habit of almost pulling the rod off its rest. What happens is that as the fish picks up the bait and turns, the weight of the feeder is sufficient to set the hook; the hooked fish then tears off upstream. When this happens, there is no need to strike because the hook is already set. As the winter wears on and the water gets colder, the fish are reluctant to move quite so much and bites become more finicky, so you do not need to use so much bait. As a rule of thumb, I would expect to use as much as 1 gal (4.50 litres) of maggots on a summer outing, but only 2 pt (1 litre) in the winter. The fish are not as tightly shoaled in the winter months, nor do they feed so actively.

The barbel is possibly the most exciting species to inhabit our rivers in real numbers, and, if you choose to fish a swim where they are present, a good day's fishing is assured.

Average size: 2-6 lb (0.9-3 kg)
British record: 13 lb 12 oz (6 kg 237 g)
J. Day 1962; Royalty Fishery, Hampshire Avon

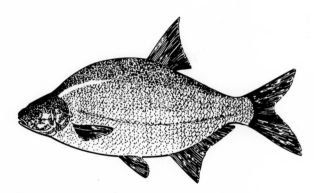

Bronze bream *Abramis brama*

Unlike barbel, bream are seldom found in hard-running water; they prefer slow-moving or still-water. They are shoaling fish and can be the easiest of all the coarse fish to catch when they are in a mood to feed, but they can also be the most elusive.

If I had to fish for one species of fish for the rest of my life, I am certain that I would choose bream. They do not fight like barbel or carp, but they are certainly the most unpredictable. They can be feeding happily in your swim, but one mistake, such as an ill-timed ball of groundbait, and they are gone, unlikely to return again.

Because of their shape - they tend to be plate shaped - they are not fierce fighters; expect a slow dogged fight rather than the violent surges of a chub. It is the pursuit of bream that makes them exciting and they are seldom caught by accident in lakes or rivers. Because of their cautious nature they prefer the security of the deeper water often found well away from the bank and for this reason, the angler who wishes to catch bream must often fish for them to the exclusion of other fish.

Bream are patrolling fish. Often they will be seen rolling in one part of a lake, only to be seen an hour later 110 yd (100 m) further on. However, their movements are not indiscriminate; careful observation will show that they tend to follow the same patrol routes each day, and if bream are to be caught in any quantity, this factor must be recognized.

At Coombe Abbey lake, one of the most prolific bream waters in the country, bream are often caught during the day along what is known as the Lindley bank, but invariably by mid-afternoon most of the fish will have drifted into the bay by the boat house. I have fished at Coombe since 1975 and I cannot recall a time when the fish did not end the day near this spot. That isn't to say that they can always be caught, simply that they are always there.

If you are going to fish for bream, location is the key. Unlike other species, bream can be observed because they tend to roll on the surface. Why they do this we do not know, for there is little to suggest that they are surface feeders. If you decide to fish for bream, try to spend some time locating the patrol route; the best time is in the evening when the water is flat. Bear in mind also that it is possible that, as the day wears on, the fish will venture nearer the bank, and it will be much easier to fish and feed at 27 yd (25 m) than it is at 66 yd (60 m).

If you do observe bream in a particular spot in the evening, it is unlikely that you will catch them there at other times of the day. Graham Marsden, a dedicated bream angler, fishes a mere in Cheshire which holds a shoal of large bream. He tells me that from the peg he fishes, it is unusual for him to get a bite before 11.30 pm, but having had his first bite the fish will continue to feed until first light before moving off again.

The secret with bream fishing, accepting that fish will, during the course of the day, pass through your swim, is to ensure that you have enough feed on the bottom to stop the shoal as they pass; one ball of groundbait or a swim-feeder won't hold thirty or forty fish for very long.

Correct groundbaiting for bream is possibly the most crucial factor in their capture; an ill-timed ball or the use of poor groundbait can spell disaster. This is covered in detail in the chapter on feeding; suffice to say here that it is crucial.

Since the development of the swingtip and latterly the quiver and springtip, bite indication on legered baits has improved out of all recognition. Many specimen anglers still insist on using dough-bobbins and such like, but quite frankly they are being short-sighted in trying to hold on to a tradition and a method which are

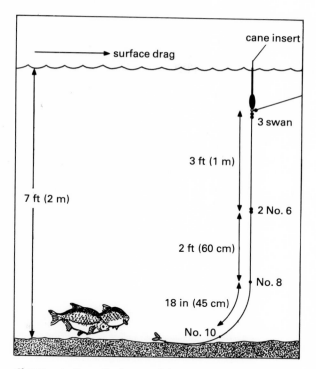

Shotting pattern for bream fishing.

inefficient and out-dated. The spring quiver is without doubt the most efficient stillwater bite indicator on the market today. The fact that anglers of the calibre of Ivan Marks, Roy Marlow and Tom Bedder are now using this method is recommendation in itself. On slow-moving water the quivertip is unbeatable.

Bream are unpredictable and, while they seem to prefer a stationary bait, will sometimes take a moving bait. Then the big float is called for. This to my mind is bream fishing at its most exciting; legering is fun, but having put in your feed and cast out, it's very often a question of patience. With the float, much more skill is required, especially if the fish are 25-30 yd (25-30 m) out from the bank.

A 2.6 or 3 lb (1.20 or 1.40 kg) reel line is needed with a 1.7 lb (0.77 kg) hook length and a bodied waggler carrying 3 swan shot. Most of the shot is placed immediately around the float to give the maximum casting distance. On the line I place a No. 10 shot 9 in (22 cm) from the

Opposite: Two bream of over 8 lb (3.6 kg). Very few anglers will manage two such specimens in a single sitting.

hook, which will drag over the bottom and steady the bait; 18 in (45 cm) above that I place a No. 8 shot and 24 in (60 cm) above that two No. 6 shot. I then cast out beyond the baited area. This has a double effect; firstly, my float is not landing directly on top of feeding fish; and secondly I can, merely by dropping my rod end into the water, reel my float back to the baited area, sinking my line as I do. When you are fishing at this distance it is crucial that you do this, as a bow quickly develops, dragging your float away from the baited area.

Like barbel, the bream is predominantly a summer species. They will take most baits, including maggots, casters, worms and bread, although bread seems to be at its most effective during the early part of the season. If you can catch them in the right mood it is possible to catch a netful, but you could return to the same spot the very next day and never get a bite.

Average size: 2-4 lb (0.9-1.80 kg)
British record: 16 lb 6 oz (7 kg 427 g)
A. Bromley 1986; Private Fishery, Staffordshire

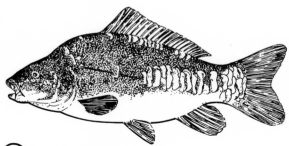

Carp *Cyprinis carpio*

There are four main species of carp found in our water. Crucian carp attract very little real attention, although they are great fun to catch, but grow only to 2 lb (900 g) or 3 lb (1.30 kg). The mirror carp, leather carp and common carp, on the other hand, attain enormous proportions, with fish in excess of 30 lb (13.50 kg) being caught each year.

Since the capture of the record carp by Richard Walker in 1952, something of a cult following has sprung up around the species, with secret baits being developed by anglers fishing on secret waters. In fact, such is the prestige attached to the capture of a 30 lb (13.50 kg) carp that anglers will pay as much as £100 per year for the privilege of fishing a water which holds such a fish. There is, however, a number of club-controlled waters which contain large species of carp. Layer Pits, near Colchester is such an example, but these waters are few and far between. Most waters containing big carp, and by that I mean fish in excess of 10 lb (4.50 kg), tend to be controlled by private syndicates. These are difficult for the average angler to join, but not impossible, and some advice on how to join is given in the chapter on specimen hunting.

The attraction of carp, with their thick-set bronzed bodies, is that they are spectacular fighters. Even the smaller 4-6 lb (1.8-3 kg) fish will offer tremendous sport to the angler fishing with light line. They are also highly intelligent fish and because of this carp baits have been developed to a most sophisticated level, with high proteins and amino acids being used. In fact certain baits that are now being used by anglers need to be taken to the water's edge in an ice-box, but this is generally on waters that contain very large fish which have been caught before. On waters that contain smaller fish, most baits are acceptable: maggots, worms, casters, bread and in recent times sweetcorn. The latter has possibly accounted for more specimen fish than any other bait, and certainly carp to 20 lb (9 kg) have been taken on it. It is perhaps fair to say that it is losing some of its seemingly magical appeal now, but is nevertheless still a marvellous bait, being easy to use and cheap to purchase.

I will deal here with fish in the 4-10 lb (1.80-4.50 kg) bracket. For these are the fish that the average angler is likely to encounter. If you plan to fish for carp, ensure that you tackle up with the proper equipment. Most reputable companies manufacture a good range of carp rods, which are suitable for catching fish up to 10 lb (4.50 kg). If, however, you feel that you wish to specialize, it is worth purchasing a rod from one of the companies making rods for the big fish specialists - companies like Terry Eustace, Alan Brown or Going Brothers. It is possible that you will pay a little more for your rod, but,

when the opportunity arises to fish for a really big specimen, your tackle will be up to the job.

I can think of few waters where it is possible to catch a netful of carp, particularly the larger ones 10 lb (4.50 kg). Two or three fish in this category would represent a good day's fishing, so that our feeding pattern must be different from the 'little and often' type we would use were we fishing for roach or chub. With the exception of the River Trent there are very few rivers which offer the carp angler the promise of any real sport. Accepting that most carp fishing is restricted to still waters, remember that whatever feed is put into a lake stays in the lake, so ensure that the swim is fed correctly.

Some years ago 'scatter baiting' became very popular. Anglers found that by scattering a new bait all over a lake, for maybe a week or ten days, they could lure the carp on to that bait. The method worked in theory, but it was expensive and time consuming, and really, had they introduced the bait into a small area where the fish were known to be, in my opinion, the method would have been much more successful. Because the fish liked the new bait - and one presumes that they would not have eaten it had they not liked it - it makes sense to assume that they would have been drawn in numbers to the area where the new bait was being introduced. I cannot subscribe to any theory which involves spreading fish throughout a lake; the basis of all fishing is to make the fish compete for food in a confined area.

Because we are fishing for larger and, there is much evidence to show, more intelligent fish, bait presentation is crucial, so always when fishing for carp, ensure that the bait you are using dictates the size of hook you use. You are still fishing for bites, because if you don't get a bite you cannot catch a fish. If you are using maggots, don't try to get eight on a size 10 hook, just because that's the hook you were using with another bait; maggots don't crawl around the bottom in eights. I know anglers have caught fish using bunches of maggots, but far more fish have been caught by anglers using one or two on the hook. When a carp moves into a swim baited with either maggots or sweetcorn, the bait will be lying perfectly natu-

Carp.

Overleaf: *Chub*.

rally on the bottom. If they are cautious of that particular bait, they are far more likely to be suspicious of a great clump of maggots than they are of one or two, so try to make your hookbait as inconspicuous as possible.

The same applies to line; 4 or 5 lb (1.80 or 2.25 kg) breaking strain line will cope with any fish up to 10 lb (4.50 kg), provided that there are no snags in the swim you are fishing. Don't be stereotyped; I know many anglers who fish with 6 lb (2.70 kg) line regardless of the swim. Always fish as fine a line as possible, without being reckless. Fine line is more subtle than thick line; fish often suck a bait into their

mouths from 4-5 in (10-12 cm) away, and two maggots on a size 16 hook to 3 lb (1.35 kg) line will move much more naturally than eight maggots on 8 lb (3.50 kg) line.

Assuming that you have access to a water which holds a good head of carp, it really can be fun fishing. There is no mystique about carp; they are wild creatures that need to feed to live, but they are not stupid, so give some thought to your approach and you will be successful.

Average size: 4-8 lb (1.8-3.6 kg)
British record: 44 lb (19 kg 957 g) Richard Walker 1952: Redmire Pool

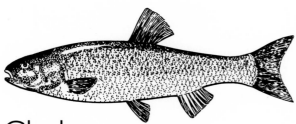

Chub *Leuciscus cephalus*

Although chub have been introduced quite successfully into a number of stillwaters, they are fundamentally river fish. Unlike other species which tend to colonize in certain types of water, however, chub can be found in all types of water from the fast-flowing Hampshire Avon to the virtually still River Welland. They abound in small streams but are equally at home on big rivers like the Trent and the Wye. There is one thing you can be certain of; if there is a snag or a fallen tree, there will be chub close by.

The great beauty of this species is that they will feed throughout the year, falling to maggots, casters, hemp, worms, bread, crayfish, wasp grub, snails, cheese and slugs. They can be fished on almost any method, including float, leger, swimfeeder or freelined. However, having said that, they can also be most elusive, particularly the bigger specimens.

Because of the diverse waters which hold chub and the many and varied methods which can be used to catch them, it is impossible to write about a specific approach.

To catch big chub in any numbers requires stealth and patience. Ask any specimen hunter how you go about catching a four pounder and he's likely to tell you to find your fish first. Because of the chub's habit of living in snags and under overhanging trees it is possible, especially in the smaller rivers like the Cherwell and the Hampshire Avon, to cast to a specific fish.

If your thoughts are on catching big chub, stout tackle is the order of the day; an Avon-type rod and 4 lb or 5 lb (1.80 or 2.25 kg) line are advisable. For me, the most enjoyable method is trotting a float close to the bank. Small chub are shoaling fish, and those in the 1-2 lb (450-900 g) class can offer great sport when fished for on match tackle. Maggots and

casters are generally the most productive bait for this type of fishing.

Average size: 1-2½ lb (.45-1.10 kg)
British record: 7 lb 6 oz (3 kg 345 g)
W. L. Warren 1957; Royalty Fishery, Hampshire Avon

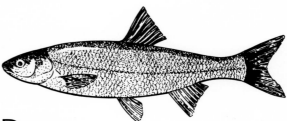

Dace *Leuciscus leuciscus*

Dace are often mistaken for small chub and whilst it is possible to identify them by their concave fins (chub have convex fins) dace tend to have much smaller mouths than chub of a similar size. Found in fast-running waters, dace are fun fish. A dace weighing 1 lb (450 g) is in fact a specimen-sized fish but it is quantity rather than quality that counts with this species. Locate a shoal, loose feed maggots and the sport is fast and furious on float-fished tackle. Because of their size, small baits like bread punch, casters and maggots are the most productive bait.

They are winter fish and will feed in the coldest weather. Fine tackle is the order of the day; a match rod, (2 lb 0.90 kg) line and small hooks, size 16 or 18.

Average size: 3-4 oz (85-115g)
British record: 1 lb 4 oz 4 drm (574 g)
J. L. Gasson 1960; Little Ouse, Thetford, Norfolk

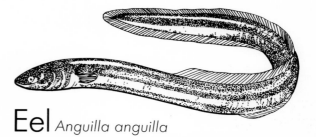

Eel *Anguilla anguilla*

After leaving the Atlantic, where it is born, the eel enters our rivers as an elver, where it stays

Eel.

for many years, before returning to the Sargasso Sea to spawn.

The eel is a much-maligned species of fish that will feed on almost anything. Small eels can be found in almost all of our rivers and many stillwaters. Whilst large eels are sought by specimen hunters, small eels often tend to be a nuisance, picking up baits intended for other fish, particularly on the Fenland waters where worm is a favourite bait with bream anglers.

Like chub, eels are great lovers of snags, and because of this you will need stout tackle when you are fishing for them. A pike rod is ideal; line of 8-10 lb (3.50-4.50 kg) is advisable, with bunches of worms fished on a size 6 or 8 hook being the most productive bait. For the larger species 5 lb (2.20 kg), location is the key, for not all lakes that hold small eels necessarily hold large ones. Many living in rivers return to the Sargasso Sea before they attain large proportions, and while a number may remain in the river it is impossible to fish with a bait that will attract 5 lb (2.20 kg) fish and not 2 lb (900 g) ones. Therefore, if you wish to catch large eels, it is important to establish that such fish exist in the waters which you are fishing.

For large eels, dead baits have proved a most successful method, but remember that unlike the other predators, pike and zander, eels have a comparatively small mouth, so portions of fish, rather than whole fish tend to be more successful.

Much has been written about when is the best time to strike, when using dead baits. The humane answer is immediately a run occurs. This will result in some fish lost, but it means that the fish caught should be hooked in the mouth. It is never an easy job to remove hooks from a deep-hooked eel, even for an expert. Eels, like all other fish, should be handled with the utmost respect and returned to their environment alive, and a deep-hooked eel is almost certainly a dead eel. The longer a run is left to develop the more chance there is of the hook being in the eel's throat. By using fish portions it is probable that, as soon as the eel picks up the bait, the hooks are in its mouth, so strike.

In recent times a number of anglers have been successful in their pursuit of big eels by groundbaiting with all manner of things, including minced fish, dried blood and chicken offal. I have mixed feelings about this practice. On the one hand, throughout this book, I advocate the importance of correct feeding and certainly this method of feeding has produced results. On the other hand, I cannot believe that this kind of feeding has anything but an adverse effect on the roach or bream which may have been present in that swim before the feed was introduced. My mixed feelings stem from the belief that one man's fishing should never lessen the next man's chances of catching fish, although I must say that I have no real evidence to suggest that this does happen.

For reasons which I have never fully understood many anglers have an aversion to eels. They are, nevertheless, an important part of the fish chain so treat them with respect.

Average size: 1-2 lb (450-900 g)
British record: 11 lb 2 oz (5 kg 46 g)
S. Terry 1978; Kingfisher Lake, near Ringwood, Hampshire

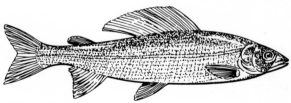

Grayling *Thymallus thymallus*

Known affectionately as the 'lady of the stream', the grayling is a beautifully marked fish. Living in fast, clear water, it is found only in the northwest of England, Scotland and a few chalk streams in the southwest of England.

Grayling fishing comes into its own in the winter months and whilst grayling can be caught both on dry and wet fly, they will respond just as willingly to maggots trotted under a float.

Average size: 10-12 oz (285-340 g)
British record: 3 lb 10 oz (1 kg 644 g)
I. White 1983; River Allen, Dorset

Gudgeon *Gobio gobio*

The canal angler's friend, gudgeon live in all types of water, but seem to be most prolific in the canals. Weighing only a few ounces, gudgeon offer little in the way of real sport except for the canal match angler, who is content to fish for them during the winter months, when as little as 1 lb (450 g) of fish can win a match.

There is evidence to suggest that gudgeon do not live very long, as they seem to appear in a river in vast quantities, and three or four years later they disappear.

Because of their size, gudgeon are best fished for on fine tackle, small hooks size 18 or 20 and small baits, such as maggots, pinkies and squatts.

Average size: 1-2 oz (30-55 g)
British record: 4 oz 4 drm (120 g)
M.J.Bowen 1977; Fish Pond, Ebbw Vale, Gwent, Wales

Perch *Perca fluviatilis*

This was once one of the most popular species of fish in our waters, but since the perch disease began to take its toll in the early 1970s, we have seen an alarming decline in this delightful species.

Perch are predators and can be caught throughout the year. They will respond to all manner of methods: dead bait, live baits, float fishing and legering. A shoaling fish, small perch can be caught on the crudest of tackle, but as they grow, they become harder to catch.

A 12 ft or13 ft (3.65 m or 3.95 m) float rod and 2 lb (1.10 kg) line are adequate to deal with most perch, although fish in the 3-4 lb (1.30-1.80 kg) class will call for sturdier tackle. Worm is a favourite bait, although caster and maggot can be killing baits.

Average size: 6-8 oz (170-225 g)
British record: 5 lb 9 oz (2 kg 523 g)
J. Shayler 1985; from Private Lake, Kent

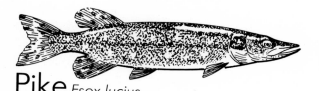

Pike *Esox lucius*

The pike, with its long, tapered body, is built for speed, and it is the largest of all the predatory fish to inhabit our waters. Pike can be found in every river and most lakes and ponds. It is a much-maligned species that many anglers, quite wrongly, blame for the decline of fisheries. In reality, this is seldom the case. In fact, pike often improve a fishery because they will eat dead and diseased fish.

There is some conjecture as to exactly how much the pike actually eats. What is known is that it will take a live or dead bait, fished either on the bottom or in mid-water. Most pike anglers prefer a bait in the 3-4 oz (85-115 g) class, but pike have been caught on baits much larger than that. Favourite baits are roach, bream, crucian carp, chub and dace. In the summer months spinning with spoons, plugs and spinners is very popular. Pike can be caught all the year round but anyone attempting it should ensure that his tackle is sturdy enough. A pike rod is required, 10 lb (4.50 kg) line, wire traces and some well-honed treble hooks.

The pike angler seldom expects to catch anything other than pike, except in the Fenland area where the recently introduced zander will respond to similar methods. It is very much specialist fishing, and is dealt with in detail in Chapter 11.

Average size: 5-10 lb (2.20-4.50 kg)
British record: 42 lb (19 kg 50g)
D. N. Amies 1985; Thurne System, Norfolk

Previous page: *a net of beautifully marked grayling.*   Above: *Two specimen roach from the Hampshire Avon.*

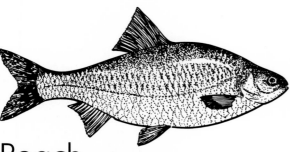

Roach *Rutilus rutilus*

This delightful fish is the most common and most fished for species of fish in our waters. Roach respond best to a float-fished bait although many specimen-sized fish are caught on legered bread. They are shoaling fish that can offer a good day's fishing, and which fight well. They can be persuaded to feed on the coldest of days.

Light match tackle is most suitable for roach fishing. 2lb (0.90 kg) line, stick float or waggler, light shotting, small hooks, size 16 or 18, and loose-fed casters or maggots will generally bring them on to feed especially as the year wears on. They are at their best during the

months of September and October, but they will feed throughout the winter.

Average size: 4-6 oz (115-170 g)
British record: 4 lb 1 oz (1 kg 842 g)
R. G. Jones 1975; Gravel Pit, Nottinghamshire

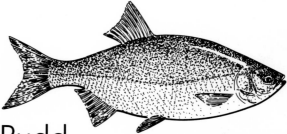

Rudd *Scardinius erythrophthalmus*

Rudd are widespread, but are not often fished for because of their nomadic tendencies. They seldom feed on the bottom and are generally caught on the drop or in mid-water. The problem is that they will seldom settle in an area long enough for anglers to catch many. One minute there is a feeding shoal in front of you and just as quickly they are gone, only to re-appear an hour later.

They are most attractive-looking fish, with a golden tinge that becomes more pronounced as the fish grows larger. They are often found living in or around weed beds. As in roach fishing, light tackle is called for if the best results are to be achieved; a very lightly shotted float should be ideal.

Average size: 4-6 oz (115-170 g)
British record: 4 lb 10oz (2 kg 97g)
D. Webb 1986; Pitsford Reservoir, Northamptonshire

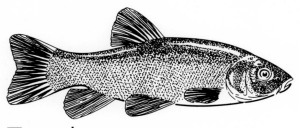

Tench *Tinca tinca*

Of all the coarse fish, the tench is perhaps the one for which all anglers feel a great affection. It is a very beautiful fish, with its smooth olive green scales, its large fins and small red eyes. Tench fishing is synonymous with balmy summer evenings, for this is the time when tench are caught. Seldom caught during the winter months, tench abound in the summer, when the water temperature is at it highest. I have read many times that tench bury themselves in the winter, but in fact, I believe that, like carp, their metabolism slows right down, so their movement and need to feed is at a minimum. I have certainly never seen any evidence to suggest that they bury themselves.

Traditionally associated with stillwaters, tench thrive quite happily in most of our rivers, but it is in lakes and ponds that they are mainly pursued.

For many years, in fact until the early 1970s, a 6 lb (2.70 kg) tench was looked upon as massive, but then, for no explainable reason, many of the specialist tench anglers began catching tench of 7 lb, 8 lb and even the odd 9 lb (3.10, 3.60 and 4 kg) fish, and then in 1975, a fish of 10 lb 1 oz 2 drm (4 kg 567 g) was taken: a new British record.

The cause of this sudden appearance of large tench has been the subject of much debate. Could it be that fish of that size have always been present, but anglers were unable to catch them? There is some evidence to suggest that this may be a possibility. As carp fishing has become more and more expensive and in the opinion of many anglers, less fun, many of the top carp men have turned their attention to tench. The Tenchfishers, a group of anglers dedicated to the pursuit of tench, have made giant steps in understanding the species and in uncovering waters which hold big tench.

Also, until quite recently it was generally felt that most coarse fish spawned each year but there is now evidence to show that this is not the case. In fact, because of the conditions which prevailed during the early 1970s, we now believe that very little spawning took place during that period. This being the case, there would be less competition for food, and consequently the fish present at that time would benefit greatly.

Like bream, tench are wandering fish, but rather than seeking the deep water away from the water's edge, they love to forage in the marginal weed which abounds during the summer months. They are bottom feeders, and tend to feed rather like the action of a vacuum cleaner, sucking in algae and insects off the bottom, eating that which they desire and blowing out that which they do not. Although it is possible to catch tench throughout the day there do seem to be marked increases in their desire to feed early in the morning around dawn and late in the evening. Like carp, they will feed on most angler's baits, but they have in recent years shown a distinct liking for sweetcorn; and bread is also a favourite bait.

Because tench show a liking for weeds, stout tackle is called for, in the form of a powerful rod and line to suit the occasion. They are strong-fighting fish, and seldom come to the net easily.

Average size: 2-4 lb (.9-1.80 kg)
British record: 12 lb 8 oz 11 drm (5 kg 689 g)
A.Wilson 1985; Wilstone Reservoir, Tring

Zander.

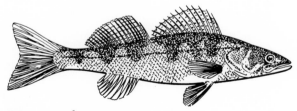

Zander *Lucioperca lucioperca*

The first zander were introduced into the land-locked Woburn Abbey lake in 1878, but they did not at that time seem to acclimatize particularly well to our water. In 1963, 97 fingerlings were introduced into the Great Ouse Relief Channel and were thus given the opportunity

Opposite: *Specialist angler, David Ball, poses with a 6-lb (2.7-kg)+ tench.*

of escaping from man's control. The spread of zander has been prolific, so much so, that it is claimed that, in their search for food, they have wiped out complete fisheries in the East Anglian region.

Unlike pike, zander are shoaling fish that hunt in packs. They show a preference for small fish, tearing into shoals of skimmer bream. Most anglers fishing for zander in East Anglia tend to employ similar tactics to those used when pike fishing, but scaling down both hooks and bait size.

Average size: 3-4 lb (1.30-1.80 kg)
British record: 17 lb 4 oz (7 kg 824 g)
D. Litton 1977; Great Ouse Relief Channel

4
FLOATS AND FLOAT FISHING

Of all the methods at the angler's disposal, the one that gives the most satisfaction and requires the most skill is float fishing, especially on moving waters like the Trent, where the top float anglers are looked upon as true artists. Unlike legering or swimfeeder fishing, where the bait is stationary, the moving bait needs to be controlled if it is to be effective. The stick float and waggler are often fished on gossamer-thin monofilament line, and in the hands of a novice can be a nightmare, but in the hands of the expert they can yield fish after fish.

As a boy living in Manchester, my fishing was limited to the local park lake, until one day an uncle took me to the Trent at Long Higgin. The river was deep and wide and the wind blew downstream. I spent the day watching my float drift round in the current and I was cold; I did not enjoy myself. On the way home my uncle commiserated with me, then he said something that did not mean very much to me at the time, 'Once you learn to fish a float properly you will never want to do anything else'; how true that is.

It was some years before I was to float fish a river again. This time it was the River Dane at Holmes Chapel in Cheshire. I caught a chub of about 1 lb (450 g) and I was hooked. After that the twenty-mile bicycle ride from Manchester did not seem so bad. Slowly I began to understand rivers, why the fish live in some parts and not in others; I discovered the loose float (they weren't called wagglers in those days); I could fish under the trees on the far bank, something I had never been able to do before. I went back to the Trent in my teens and won club matches.

I bought my first fixed-spool reel - that was a magical experience. I could cast a float to the middle of the Trent if I wanted to, but there were no fish in the middle then.

On the occasional weekend when I am not fishing, I take my sons for a walk round Daventry reservoir, a popular day-ticket water close to my home. It is a nice water, full of roach and skimmer bream, but it is deep, and how the anglers struggle, many using the wrong type of float. They have shots strung out all over the place, and they don't have enough line on their reels: just like myself all those years ago on the Trent. The only difference, it seems to me, is that I wanted to improve, whereas many anglers I meet seem content to soldier on, accepting dry nets and line tangles as an occupational hazard - but that need not be the case. I cannot imagine myself going pleasure fishing and not catching fish, simply because I can pick my venue, often the very spot that I want to fish and the species that I want to fish for. And a pleasure trip for me invariably means a day's float fishing.

It amazes me, when I consider the number of words written on the subject of angling, that so many anglers simply do not understand what specific floats are intended to do. I see anglers fishing balsa floats on lakes and wagglers being fished with a top rubber. Of course not all anglers are so ill-informed; and the young, especially, strive constantly for improvement.

If you want to improve your float fishing techniques, it is crucial, first of all, that you understand your float box: why an inserted waggler will work one day and not the next;

The author float fishing on the River Severn at Holt Fleet in Worcestershire.

when to fish with shot strung out on the line, and when to bunch it; what the difference is between a peacock insert and a cane insert. All of this and much more must be learned before you can call yourself a float angler.

There are essentially two types of float: those which are attached to the line top and bottom - they are stick floats and balsas; and those which are fixed through the bottom eye only - these are wagglers. In a nutshell, floats fixed top and bottom are for use on moving waters only; wagglers, on the other hand, can be used on still and slow-moving waters.

To explain when and where each float should be used would in itself fill a book, especially when you consider how many floats there are on the market. Many of them do not perform the function for which they are intended; in fact, I would go so far as to suggest that as many as 50 per cent of the floats sold in this country are of no use whatsoever to the angler. A dealer once said to me, 'most floats are for selling, not for using'. For that reason, I would suggest that anglers attempt to make their own floats. You will make mistakes initially; I cringe when I think back to my early efforts and even now I don't make the prettiest floats, but they perform perfectly the function for which they were designed.

Making your own floats does more than give you something to do in the evenings; it makes you think about your fishing. Let me give you an example. Two years ago I started to fish a series of matches at Mallory Park. The lake was full of skimmer bream in the 3 oz-1 lb (85-450 g) class; the bait was four squatts on a size 22 hook fished 33 yd (30 m) out. I decided to have a practice session and I finished with a good catch of fish, but on several occasions I reeled in to find my squatts had been sucked without ever seeing a bite. I tried several different floats, but I could not resolve the problem. That evening I made a float which consisted of an 8 in (20 cm) piece of peacock quill with a 3 in (7 cm) cane insert; the float shotted took 3AAA and a dust shot. The next day I went back to Mallory. I

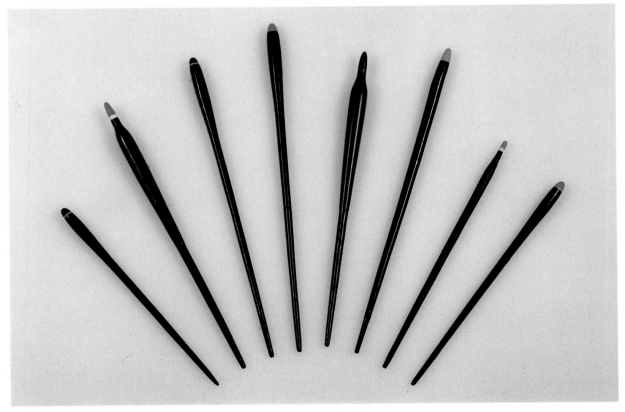

A selection of stick and balsa floats.

set my float so that the only shot on the line, the dust shot, was just dragging the bottom (the 3AAA were locked under the float). I cast in and the float settled; within minutes I had my first bite. The fish picked up my bait and in doing so it lifted the dust shot off the bottom. The effect was that the 3 in (7 cm) cane insert lifted clean out of the water and the fish was hooked. I fished eight matches at Mallory Park that year: I won two, was second twice, third once and fourth once, all because of that little float. Let me explain why I made the float that way.

It was clear to me what was happening. I had succeeded in getting the bream to feed but, unlike roach that pick up a bait and then turn with it, the skimmers were in fact picking up the bait and eating it on the spot, which meant that the float was not going under. I estimated that I was missing at least 50 per cent of the bites I was getting, so I decided that if I couldn't get the fish to pull the float under, maybe I could get them to lift it up. Hence the use of the cane insert, as cane has virtually no buoyancy at all. I set the float up in a bath at home, put a dust shot on the line, then trimmed off the top of the cane so that 3/4 in (2 cm) was showing. However, because of the cane's lack of buoyancy, once the dust shot was lifted the cane came straight out of the water.

Had I never made that float, I still would have caught fish, but I could not have caught the same number. By thinking about the problem, not only was I able to catch more fish, but I added a valuable asset to my float box; plus it gave me a tremendous amount of satisfaction.

Because anglers are compulsive purchasers of floats, they invariably carry too many, most of which they never use. Let us look at what we should carry in our float boxes, and why.

The stick float

This is the most limited, yet the most important float; master it and you are on your way to becoming a complete coarse fisherman. Designed originally by the north-west canal anglers, the stick is strictly a river float, fished top and bottom. It has no other use. Constructed of two-thirds cane and one-third balsa,

there are possibly more bad sticks on the market than any other float. The better ones are those bearing the following names: Clive Smith, Kenny Giles, Max Winters, Pete Warren or Ultra. There are others, but the five mentioned produce good floats consistently.

The stick float is the only float over which the angler has complete control in moving water. It is limited because in depths of over 10 ft (3 m),

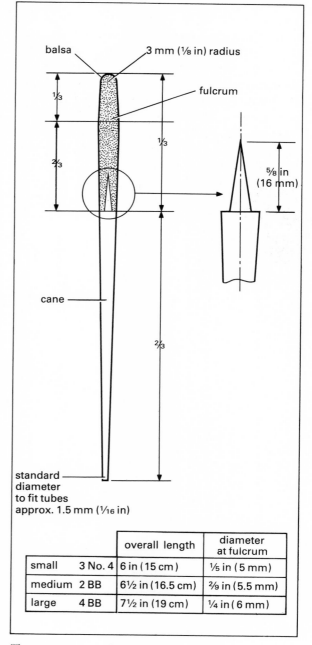

		overall length	diameter at fulcrum
small	3 No. 4	6 in (15 cm)	⅛ in (5 mm)
medium	2 BB	6½ in (16.5 cm)	²⁄₉ in (5.5 mm)
large	4 BB	7½ in (19 cm)	¼ in (6 mm)

The construction of the stick float.

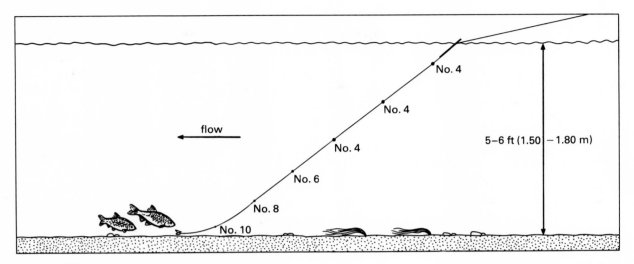

Basic stick float set-up.

or fished more than two or three rod lengths from the bank, that control is often lost and the waggler begins to come into its own. On rivers like the Trent, the Thames, the Severn and the Warwickshire Avon, where depths of 6-7 ft (1.80-2 m) can be found, with a nice steady pull, the stick float can be a winning method when fishing one rod's length from the bank.

Wind dictates how efficiently the stick can be fished. Ideally the float should be fished over depth and eased gently down the swim, keeping the line between rod tip and float - behind the float at all times. This becomes difficult when you are confronted with either a facing or a downstream wind. The most favourable wind is upstream and coming off your shoulder, because it allows you to hold the line off the water, controlling the float down your swim.

Because fish are invariably caught very close when stick float fishing, it is important that floating lines like Beyer or Racine Tortue are used, so that the strike is clean and quiet. Old or sinking lines tend to cause unnecessary disturbance. As a match angler, I tend to change my line every month, but then I fish three matches a week. Anglers fishing only once a

An open match in progress on the prolific upper stretches of the River Trent at Burton-on-Trent. This water may perhaps be the most improved fishery in Britain.

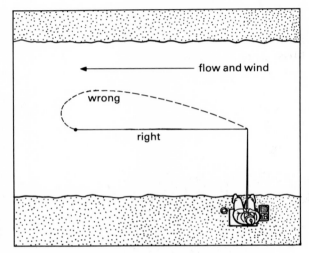

It is important to keep the line behind the float.

week need not change their lines quite so frequently, but if success is to be achieved with the stick float, it is important that this point is not overlooked.

Shotting is crucial, but sadly there are few hard and fast rules to help the novice, because depth and flow dictate what shot goes on the line. A simple guideline is: always ensure that your shots decrease in size the nearer they are to the hook.

Two further points to remember are that, unless you are experienced, never try to fish a stick in a downstream wind; and never try to fish further out than you can cast underarm as you will lose control of the float.

Balsas

Balsas are the most straightforward float, being made entirely of balsa wood. Like the stick float, they are fished top and bottom. They are made for use in fast streamy rivers like the Wye or the Ribble.

Waggler

The waggler is not in fact a float, it is the name of a type of float which principally is fished loose, locked on to the line with a shot either side of the eye. Into this category fall missiles, antennas and duckers and the main advantage that these floats have over stick floats is that they can be fished at a distance. The principal ingredients in the manufacture of wagglers is peacock quill or sarkanda reed. I have a preference for peacock because of its extra buoy-ancy, but from a float-maker's point of view, sarkanda is much easier to work because it is consistent. Two similar pieces of sarkanda will take more or less the same amount of shot, it is not quite such a simple task to match up pieces of peacock.

As I have said, the advantage of waggler floats is that they can be cast considerable dis-tances: the disadvantage is that the angler has very little real control over the float, apart from mending line, as the float fishes itself, running through the swim at the speed of the current. It cannot be held back or eased down as can the stick. Wagglers are available in a great variety of sizes, from those taking two No. 1 shot to the large-bodied types taking as much as four swan shot. It is with the bigger floats that most inex-perienced anglers get into trouble, because they tend to become confused as how best to locate so much shot on the line. I have seen

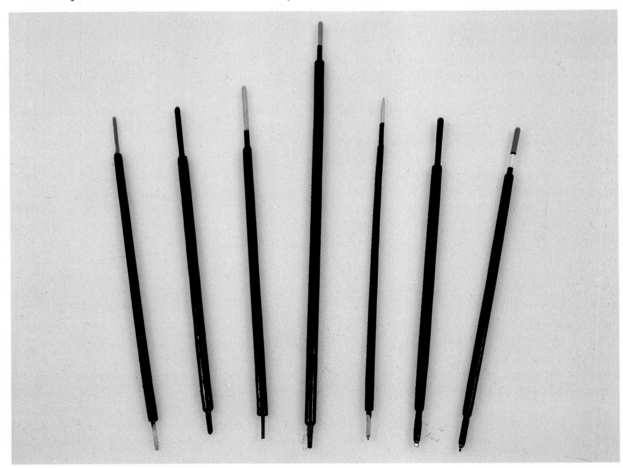

A selection of straight sarkandas and peacock wagglers.

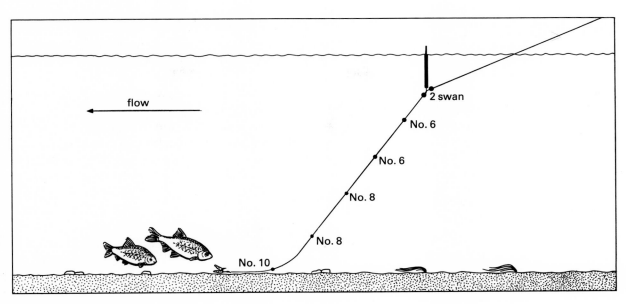

Basic waggler set-up.

anglers fishing with seven or eight BBs strung out. As with the stick float, there are no hard and fast rules about shotting, but remember that, because the waggler is fished loose, it cannot be fished in turbulent water; consequently, the need for a necklace of shot on the line is eliminated.

Shotting

In the past anglers have created all manner of fancy shotting patterns. Nowadays, however, match anglers are much more sensible in their approach. The basic shotting pattern is as follows: the bulk of the shot is placed directly underneath the float with perhaps two No. 4s 4 ft (1.20 m) from the hook, two No. 6s below that, followed by a single No. 6 and a No. 8 1ft (30 cm) from the hook. In deep water over 9 ft (2.70 m), I would normally place two No. 1s at mid-depth, just to get the bait down quicker. If I was fishing overdepth, I would probably include a No. 10 shot on my hook length, allowing this to drag the bottom, which will have the effect of steadying up the hookbait. A special shotting pattern for bream is given in Chapter 3.

It is difficult to write about shotting because, as I said earlier, conditions dictate what goes on the line and conditions change constantly. Thus it is not uncommon to change a float or a shotting pattern five or six times during the course of a five-hour match. Accepting that that can happen on a single peg in such a short period of time, it is impossible to describe a shotting pattern which will work on all manner of waters. All I would say is, always think about the shot that you put on the line. Ask yourself, 'Why am I putting that shot there?' If you cannot find an explanation, take it off.

Choice of waggler

I am often amazed when I speak to anglers about the floats that they are using, for clearly many do not relate what they are trying to achieve with the float they are using. Choice of float is dictated by where the fish are (how far out), depth, wind and flow. If, on a stillwater, the surface water is moving in the opposite direction to the natural drift, then a float long enough to get under the surface drift is called for; if bites are shy, then a cane or reed insert is called for. Waggler fishing is easy if you think about the job in hand.

There is a number of floats which, while essentially wagglers, have at some time been designed to fulfil a specific function and consequently have a special name. The missile, for example, is a large-bodied waggler loaded with a brass insert. It was designed some years ago by the Coventry anglers to beat the bad winds

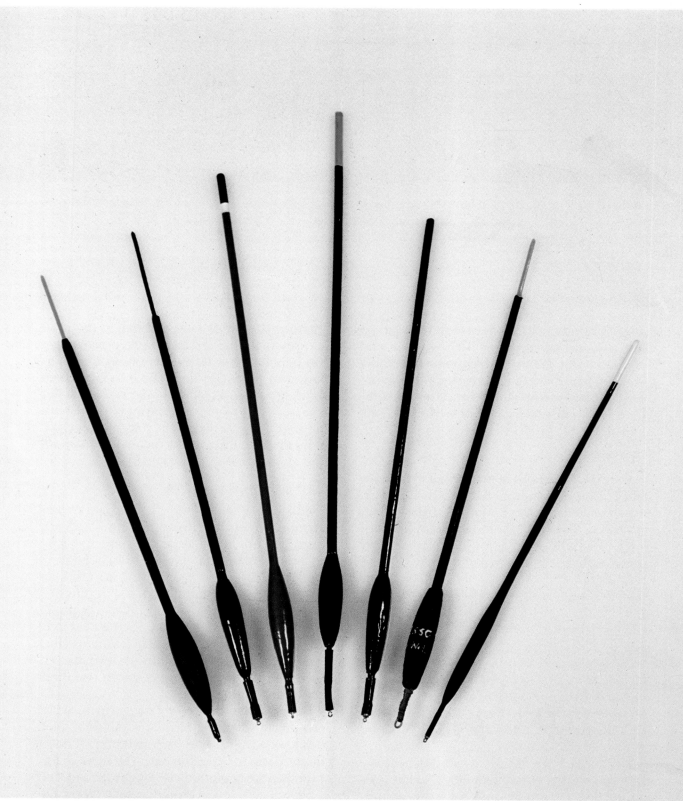

A selection of bodied wagglers.

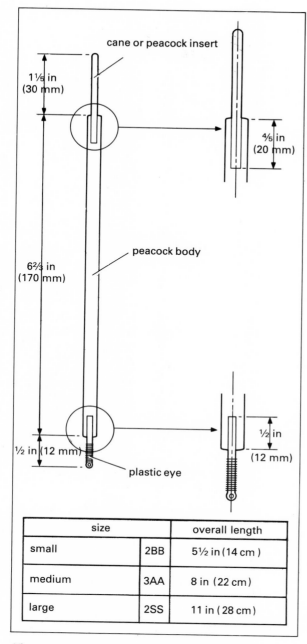

cane or peacock insert

1⅛ in
(30 mm)

⅘ in
(20 mm)

peacock body

6⅔ in
(170 mm)

½ in (12 mm)

plastic eye

½ in
(12 mm)

size		overall length
small	2BB	5½ in (14 cm)
medium	3AA	8 in (22 cm)
large	2SS	11 in (28 cm)

The construction of the waggler showing the proportions of the different elements of which it is composed.

on the Relief Channel. The zoomer is another loaded-bodied waggler designed by Ivan Marks and the 'Likely Lads'. It is perhaps the only waggler type float that is fished top and bottom. This float was responsible for Ivan, Dave Downes, Roy Marlow and Dave Rossi winning many matches on the Welland and the Nene; but that was in the days before legering became the sophisticated method that it is today. The zoomer is seldom used these days. The ducker is simply a bodied waggler.

In some respects angling is a complicated sport because, until a few years ago, anglers in different parts of the country were using floats similar to those used elsewhere, but calling them by different names. Hence, instead of having a situation where there are four different types of waggler - straight, bodied, loaded and inserted - we have a variety of names which confuse the novice. What makes the situation even more confusing is that even the top anglers each have their own preferences; walk along a match length and the chances are that each angler's float will differ in some way from the next man's. Try not to fall into the trap of having favourite floats; keep an open mind and try always to choose the float which is best suited to the job in hand.

There is a number of other types of float on the market which I do not intend to get involved with at this time, for two reasons. Firstly, the three types of float that I have mentioned will, in many cases, do the job better. Secondly, so many of them, such as the Trent trotter and the slider, are limited in their usefulness and in the hands of the inexperienced angler they are seldom a killing method. Ian Heaps is the master of the sliding float, but then he is also former World Champion. Master the basics first; there is plenty of time to get involved with specialist floats later.

5
LEGERING

Until twenty-five years ago, legering was looked upon as a 'chuck it and chance it' method of fishing, but with the advent of modern bite indicators - the swingtip, quivertip and springtip - legering has become an integral part of the coarse fisherman's armoury.

Legering is primarily a method of fishing with a lead weight anchored firmly on the bottom. It is not itself a recently devised method; in fact, there is evidence to suggest that this form of fishing was practised in the days of Izaak Walton. Until quite recently, however, the fundamental problem with the method was one of bite detection. Bites were signalled by either the fish bolting and pulling the end of the angler's rod, or by the angler holding his line gently between his fingers and feeling for a biting fish (a method still employed today by certain specimen hunters). In 1957, a tackle dealer by the name of Jack Clayton devised the first swingtip, and whilst few people took the swingtip seriously at the beginning, this method was to revolutionize legering within a few years.

Legering has many advantages. The most important of which are that it allows the angler to perform two functions which cannot be performed on the float: to fish efficiently at a great distance - up to 88 yd (80 m) from the bank - and to present a still bait in moving water. These are two major advantages when fishing large reservoirs or rivers like the Welland and

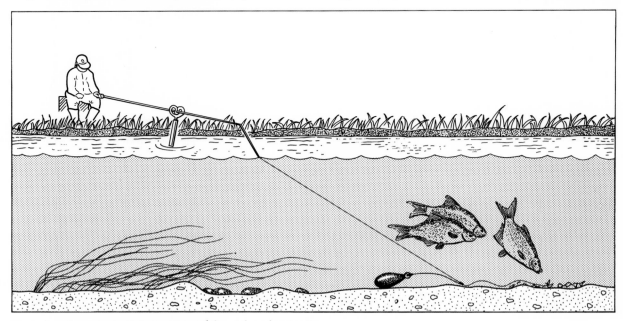

Basic legering set-up. Note position of the rod and swingtip.

the Great Ouse.

By today's standards the early swingtip was crude, but with the tremendous growth of match fishing, we have seen legering developed to a more sophisticated level, with anglers like Ivan Marks, Johnny Hart, Freddie Foster and many others adding much to its improvement. Today, it is not unusual to see anglers fishing with 7 ft (2 m) hook lengths and tiny size 20 hooks and catching bream 'on the drop'. But like so many aspects of fishing, it is the few top anglers who are getting the maximum results from the method; the pleasure angler or the less experienced angler still seems content to 'chuck it and chance it'.

Because of the society in which we live, rivers are becoming more and more polluted, and with the increasing cost of petrol, anglers are looking to fish closer to home. This often means going to the local reservoir or gravel pit, and nowhere can legering be more successful than on this type of venue. Invariably the waters are popular with anglers, particularly if they hold a good head of fish. At the weekend, every peg is taken and bankside disturbance is considerable, causing the fish to move from the margins to the sanctuary of the deeper water, often 33-44 yd (30-4 m) from the bankside. Whilst it is possible for the experienced angler to fish efficiently at this distance using a float, it is a situation that really calls for the leger, especially if the quarry is bream, for no species of fish responds better to a well-presented stationary bait than this one.

The set-up

Unlike float fishing, where a long 12 ft (3.65 m) rod is an advantage, when legering the rod will, for the most part, be positioned on a rod rest, so a 9 or 10 ft (2.75 or 3.05 m) rod is ideal. The rod should be through-actioned, allowing the angler to use fine line (2 lb/0.90 kg if he wishes); the bite indicator can be a swingtip, quivertip or a springtip. Generally I let conditions dictate which tip I use.

If conditions are good and there is not too much tow on the water I use a springtip, which I consider to be the ultimate bite indicator, sim-

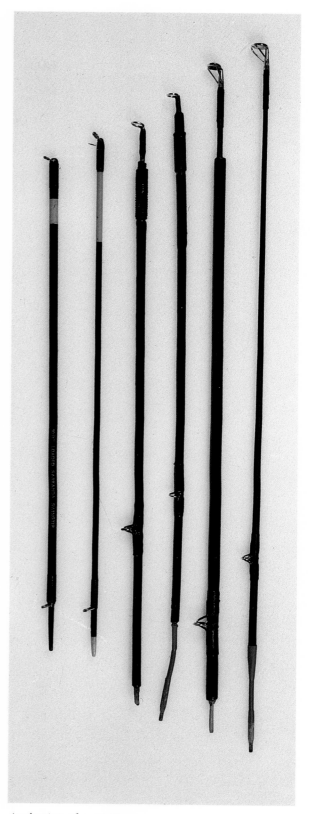

A selection of swingtips.

The author fishing with a swingtip. Note the angle of the rod.

ply because it offers no resistance to a biting fish, whereas the swingtip and the quivertip do offer an increasing amount of resistance the further they are pulled - not that this has ever proved to be a major problem. However, an indicator which offers no resistance must be better than an indicator which offers some resistance, regardless of how little, particularly on the days when the fish are finicky.

If, on the other hand, the conditions are poor, with wind and broken water, I would use a quivertip and target board combination. The target is a black board approximately 9 in (22 cm) square with a 3 in (7 cm) white band painted diagonally down the length of the board. It is affixed to a bank stick and positioned 12 in (30 cm) from the end of the rod, so that when the rod is positioned on the rest the quivertip shows up clearly against the white background; this helps considerably when the tip is being moved by high winds or waves.

If conditions are good and I am not planning to fish in excess of 49 yd (45 m) out, and I am expecting to catch a good bag of fish, I might use a swingtip; my reasoning being that whenever a situation exists where a big bag of bream

can be put together, invariably a large number of line bites is experienced. When using a springtip, which is extremely sensitive, it is very difficult to tell the difference between the real bites and the line bites. And bearing in mind how easy it is to scare bream, I am reluctant to strike at false bites as it drags the bomb across the backs of the feeding fish. Time and time again I have seen anglers strike at line bites and upset the shoal, which promptly melts to another part of the lake.

I tend to use 3 lb (1.35 kg) line for my leger fishing, but this a personal choice. Some people use a slightly heavier line, but 3 lb (1.35 kg) will handle most fish, as long as the lake or reservoir is fairly snag-free. A good open-faced fixed-spool reel is ideal; I recommend an open-faced reel because on days when there is little or no wind, it is a good policy to 'feather' the line as your bomb hits the water, causing the minimum amount of splash. It is much easier to do this with an open-faced reel than a closed-faced one.

Arlesey bombs and hook sizes are determined by the bait used and the distance fished. Bread flake, for example, is very air resistant; a

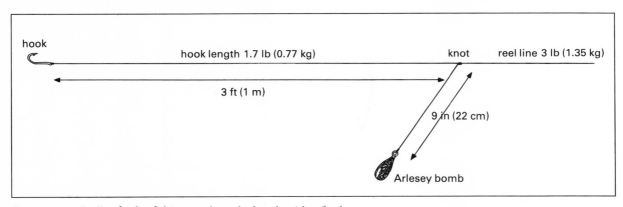

Paternoster rig. For feeder fishing, replace the bomb with a feeder.

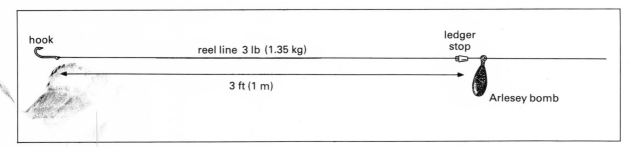

Using a sliding link.

3/8 oz (10 g) bomb will carry a maggot or worm bait 44-55 yd (40-50 m) with ease under normal conditions, yet a ½ oz (15 g) Arlesey bomb is needed to carry a piece of bread flake the same distance. Hook sizes are determined by the bait used: for bread a size 6 or 8; for maggots a size 16 or 18; and for worm a size 12 or 14. Many anglers make the mistake of allowing their hook to dictate their bait, which is short-sighted because it is not the hooks that catch the fish but the bait.

Terminal rigs

Much has been written about terminal rigs in recent years, many authors making a very simple exercise appear most complex. Without doubt the most efficient terminal rig for all leger fishing is the fixed paternoster. Without exception this is the method used by every one of the top match anglers in England, and that in itself is justification for recommending it to you. The length of line between bomb and hook is variable, but normally a 3 ft (1 m) tail is the accepted length; this can be lengthened or shortened depending on the way the fish are feeding.

The approach to the water

Unlike float fishing, which often involves a lot of movement, casting, mending line and loose feeding, legering tends to be a more relaxed method of fishing, so it is important that we position ouselves and our tackle properly. On stillwaters always try to position your rod at a 45-degree angle to the bank, with the rod tip no more than 12 in (30 cm) from the water. I often see anglers fishing with their rods pointing straight out in front of them, and whilst it is possible to see bites this way, experience has taught me that it is much easier to see bites when the rod is positioned to the side.

A common mistake made by many anglers is that they set up their tackle and then proceed to catapult five or six balls of groundbait into their chosen swim, only to find after their first cast

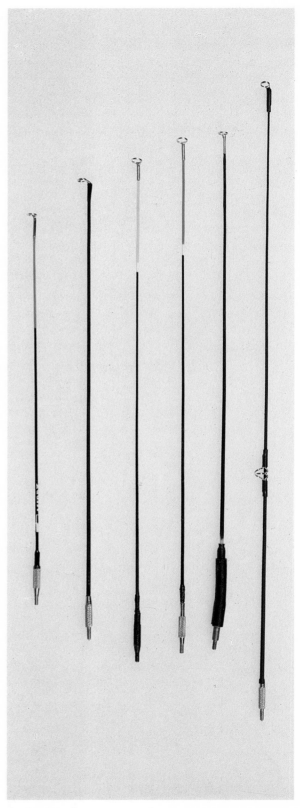

A selection of springtips and quivertips.

The quivertip and target board set-up. The parallel lines on the target board will show the angler any movement which his tip might make. Also the rod tip is seen very clearly because it is viewed against a dark background.

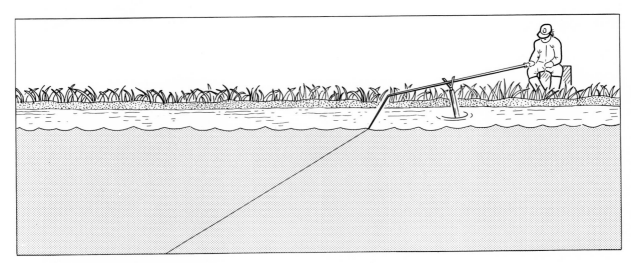

Stillwater legering. Swingtip pointing straight out into lake or stillwater.

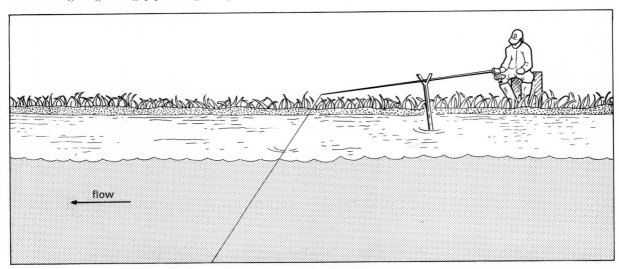

Legering in flowing water. The rod is held nearly parallel with the bank and almost always pointing downstream.

that they have put their bait into the middle of a weed bed, which is impossible to fish.

Before you start fishing, you need to establish two things: firstly, are there any snags in your chosen swim; and secondly, what is the depth? Both of these questions can be answered quite simply. Having tied your bomb directly to your 3 or 4 lb (1.35 or 1.80 kg) reel line, before tying your hook length, cast out to your chosen area; as the bomb hits the water, close your bail arm and watch your tip, counting slowly at the same time. When the bomb reaches the bottom of the lake, the tip - be it a swing, quiver or springtip - will drop back. As a rule of thumb, a 3/8 oz (10 g) bomb will nor-

mally fall at a rate of 2 ft (60 cm) per second, so if you have a count of five your chosen swim is approximately 10 ft (3 m) deep. Having satisfied yourself that the depth of water is to your liking, with your rod tip pointing down towards the water, slowly wind your bomb back towards you, this will tell you the condition of the lake bed between you and your swim. If there is a snag you may possibly lose your bomb, but better that, than waste 4-5 lb (1.80-2.20 kg) of expensive groundbait.

Opposite: *The author legering on the faster-flowing River Trent. Note how the rod is positioned to keep as much line as possible out of the water.*

Because there is no visible indicator to tell you exactly where the hookbait is lying on the lake bed, feeding when legering is rather more difficult than when float fishing. Again this is an area where anglers - through lack of thought - handicap themselves. Before your first cast, always find a marker to aim at, a tree or bush on the far bank, a buoy in the water. It is impossible to cast a bomb into a 30 acre (12 hectare) lake without a marker and then expect to be able to feed acurately; not even the best anglers in the country can do that. Always cast to a marker.

Another problem which often confronts the less experienced angler is that of tightening up to his bomb. This is caused by allowing line to spill off the spool until the bomb hits the lake bed, causing a large bow to develop in the line between the angler and his bomb. Until the line is tightened the angler is not fishing efficiently. An easy way of overcoming this problem is to over-cast your baited area by the depth you are fishing; i.e. if the lake is 10 ft (3 m) deep, you over-cast by that amount. As your bomb hits the water, close the bale arm on your reel. This will cause two things to happen: firstly, because your line is now tight to the bomb, the bomb will fall back on to your baited area; secondly, as the bomb reaches the lake bed, your tip will drop back. Two turns of the reel will take up what little slack line there is and almost immediately you are fishing efficiently.

Legering in running water

Up to now I have dealt with legering in still or slow-moving waters, but the ability to fish stationary bait can be just as effective in fast-moving rivers like the Trent, the Derwent and the Severn. The fundamental difference in approach concerns the position of the rod in the rest. Obviously the key to success in leger fishing on this type of venue is the ability to keep the bomb still in the area where the fish are feeding. It is a simple matter to cast in and allow the bomb to swing round until it takes up a stationary position, but unfortunately that is seldom where the fish are. In moving water, never be afraid to use extra lead. I have used a $1\frac{1}{2}$ oz (40 g) bomb on many occasions on the Trent. Using a paternoster rig, the fish must move your tip before it feels the lead, so the size of bomb used in no way detracts from your ability to get bites. The important thing is to keep the bait still. Another cause of bombs moving in moving water is water pressure on the line. For this reason, it is advisable to position your rod upwards on this type of water, so that you minimize the actual amount of line in the water.

For this type of venue, the quivertip is a must; there are various types on the market, but like floats many are designed to catch anglers rather than fish. The most popular quivertips are the tapered ones approximately 10 in (25 cm) in length. It pays to carry a number in differing strengths so that any eventuality can be coped with; obviously a tip which is ideal for a low sluggish river in the summer is not going to prove quite as effective when the river is carrying 3 ft (1 m) of flood water in February; so be prepared for all conditions.

In the twenty-five years since the first swingtips appeared on the match fishing scene, almost every major match has at one time or another been won by an angler legering. The former world match record catch of 161 lb 14 1/4 oz (73 kg) was taken by Leicester angler Tom Bedder, whilst legering. Richard Walker's record carp was taken whilst legering. Russell Foster won the 1976/77 National Championship using a swingtip. Whenever fish will only feed on a stationary bait, there is no known method of fishing more devastating than legering. Practise your casting, think about your feeding and you will be successful.

6

THE SWIMFEEDER

First developed many years ago, the swim-feeder - or feeder as it is commonly known - didn't really become an integral part of the angler's tackle until the mid-1970s when massive bags of barbel began to fall to the feeder/maggot combination on the River Severn. Almost overnight the feeder revolution began, first on the Severn, then the Warwickshire Avon, the Ribble, the Thames and the Trent. At the same time, the specimen hunters began using the feeder to great effect on reservoirs like Tring and the Cheshire meres.

Almost from the first time it was used in matches, there has been a move by many of the top anglers to have the feeder banned. The reason for this is that on the right peg, even in the hands of a comparative novice, it can be a match-winning method, so much so that the great Gloucester angler Max Winters once commented, 'They should give the prizes to the feeder, not the angler.'

What makes the feeder so devastating? Throughout this book I have stressed the importance of correct feeding, and the feeder is in effect a mechanical feeder. Providing an angler can cast reasonably accurately he can catch fish using the feeder because, as he has to fill the feeder physically before each cast, he ensures that a steady flow of bait is being deposited into his swim. Consequently, providing that he casts every ten minutes or so, the swim will be kept alive. In some respects I can understand why certain anglers would like to see the feeder banned, because it does create 'instant' anglers. This might not be a good thing for match angling, but anything that helps anglers catch more fish must be a good thing for the sport.

Types of feeder

In recent years we have seen many different feeders come on to the market, most of which do the job quite effectively. There are two types of feeder: the open-ended type which is used in conjunction with groundbait; and the block-end type which is designed to carry maggots.

Let us look first at the open-ended feeder. This can either be open at both ends or, as is the modern trend, open only at the bottom. This type of feeder is popular on still or slow waters where bream or tench are the quarry. The normal practice is to fill the feeder with hook samples, then plug the end with groundbait. After casting, allow a couple of minutes for the groundbait plug to soak, then give your reel a half turn, this will deposit your hookbait very close to the contents of your feeder, which will have spilled out. The beauty of the open-ended feeder is that a greater variety of baits can be used. Because of the large open end, sweet-corn or even luncheon meat can be put into the feeder.

However, on faster-moving rivers like the Severn, where very often the killing bait is maggot, or on waters where the introduction of groundbait has an adverse effect on the fishing, the blockend feeder comes into its own. This is simply filled with maggots or pinkies, which crawl out on the river bed. The feeder is simplicity itself, yet it has accounted for many, many fish and angling is about catching fish.

The top specimen hunters have modified the feeders so that they are more aerodynamic and are now fishing at distances of up to 88 yd (80 m) on the large reservoirs. The match anglers are no longer fishing 8 lb (3.50 kg) line tied direct to size 10 hooks; now it is 3 lb (1.35 kg) line, 1.7 lb (0.77 kg) hooklength and size 18 or 20 hooks; such have been the developments.

Method of fishing

Anglers are great innovators. A new method like the feeder begins to make an impact and before very long the specimen hunters are modifying it to suit their purposes, whilst at the other end of the chain the match anglers are doing likewise. But unlike other methods, the feeder can be very effective even in its simplest form.

On stillwaters a straightforward 9 ft (2.75 m) leger rod-quivertip combination is adequate,

and 3 or 4 lb (1.35 or 1.80 kg) line, depending on the size of the feeder used or the distance cast. Using the paternoster rig as described in the chapter on legering there is no reason why fish should not be caught providing, as I have already said, that the angler can cast reasonably accurately. I prefer to fish the feeder over a bed of groundbait whenever I can. This is because it is impossible to cast into exactly the same spot every time, and therefore little clumps of maggots or casters tend to be deposited around the swim. This does not induce a shoal of fish to stop, and the result is that you only catch one or two fish as the shoal passes by. If the feeder is dropped on to a bed of groundbait, I believe the whole thing becomes much more appetizing.

The feeder has proved that it can be equally if not even more devastating on moving water, especially when chub and barbel are present. The secret here is to keep the feeder still. Many

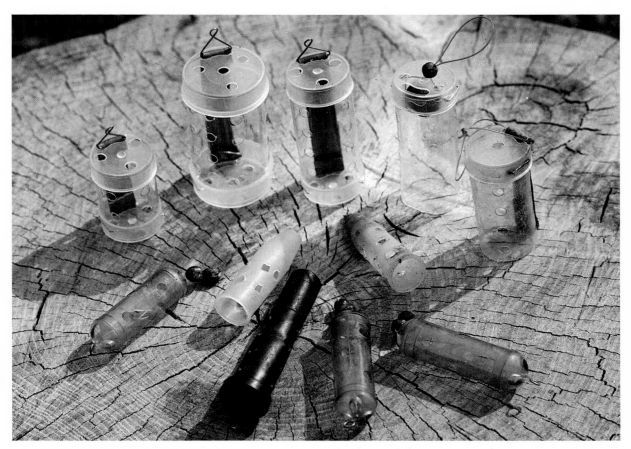

A selection of open-ended and blockend swimfeeders.

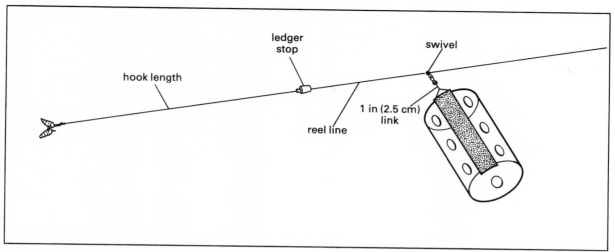

The swimfeeder on a sliding link.

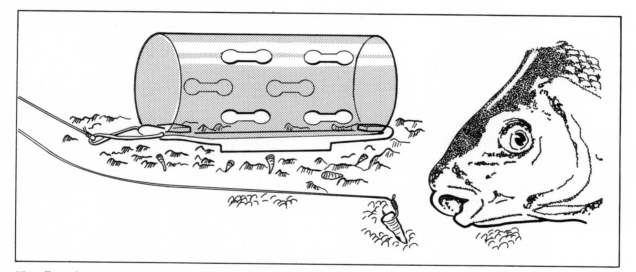

The effect of an open-ended feeder.

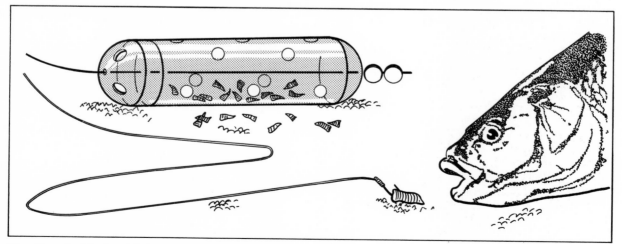

The effect of a blockend feeder.

anglers do not realize that allowing the feeder to move succeeds only in baiting up an area of river that is much too large to concentrate the fish. Furthermore, by allowing the feeder to swing round in the current, when it does eventually stop moving, it will invariably be empty, having left the contents elsewhere. Always make sure that there is enough lead on the feeder to keep it stationary in the current.

As I said earlier, most of the feeders currently on sale in the tackle shops are more than adequate, but there is not one single feeder that will cope with all the different situations that confront the angler, so you should carry a selection. Do not be afraid to experiment; both specimen hunters and match anglers have and in doing so they have increased their catches.

7
FISHING BAITS

Whilst maggots have probably accounted for more fish than any other bait, it is a foolish angler who fishes only with maggots, for although many of the other baits only work effectively at certain times in the year, they can, during that spell, prove to be devastating. And this is never more apparent than when summer fishing for roach with hemp and tares. An angler can be catching roach in the 3-4 oz (85-115 g) class on the maggot; but switch to hemp and tares and he will start catching fish in the 8 oz-1 lb (225-450 g) class, every cast.

There is a seemingly endless number of exotic baits which have accounted for fish over the years; some I have tried, many I have not. To my knowledge, that great angler Richard Walker has caught fish on such varied baits as peas, baked beans, cornflakes, puffed wheat, earwigs and caterpillars. On that basis it would appear that fish will eat almost anything - and so they will - but not all of the time. Years ago the Daventry reservoir was so full of fish that once you had them feeding, it was possible to catch fish on a bare hook. However, baits like peas, baked beans and even bare hooks are the exception rather than the rule.

Accepting that whenever we go fishing we are fishing for bites, clearly we must fish with a bait which we know will appeal to the majority of fish. There are exceptions, of course; the specimen hunter who is interested in catching only the bigger specimens will often use a bait which will prove of little interest to the smaller fish: a potato or a large piece of bread flake.

Let us look at the baits which are used most commonly and when to use them.

Maggots

Without a doubt, this is the most commonly used bait. I can think of no coarse fish that does not from time to time fall to the humble maggot. They can be used all the year round on both still and moving waters and are available in a variety of colours: red, yellow, white and bronze. In recent years the bronze maggot has proved the most productive, although I have caught many bonus fish on red ones. If the maggot has a weakness, it is that small fish have a liking for it; this is not to deny that it will account for the bigger fish if they are present, but small roach, dace and small chub have a tendency to intercept it before it gets down to the bigger fish.

Gozzers

Strictly speaking, the gozzer is the maggot produced by the woodfly, but most people these days, when talking about gozzers, are referring to fresh, home-produced maggots. Because of the demand for maggots, it is almost impossible for commercial breeders to produce really fresh maggots. Invariably, when an angler buys bait from his local tackle shop, it is at least three or four days old and during that period it will have shrunk and become tough.

Bream are the 'sucker' fish for a really soft white gozzer and as many of our rivers in the east of the country hold big shoals of bream, it is not difficult to understand why the top match anglers go to great lengths to produce a really soft maggot.

Fresh, home-bred gozzers.

Breeding gozzers at home is a simple exercise. Buy a small piece of chicken or a lamb's heart and place it in a biscuit tin or a similar container, and lightly cover it with a crumpled newspaper. Place the container under a shed or hedge and leave it. Obviously the breeding of gozzers at home is limited to the summer months, when there is an abundance of flies around, but even during this period it can sometimes take all day for a blow to materialize. When you have succeeded in getting a blow, wrap the meat in two or three sheets of newspaper, put it back in the container and top up with fresh bran (this eliminates the possibility of any odour). Cover the container and place it in the corner of your shed. Now leave it alone; continually opening it will do nothing to enhance the finished gozzer. After seven days, tip the contents on to a riddle and you will find that the gozzers have now come off the feed and should run through quite quickly. Now place the fresh gozzers into a clean container, cover with damp bran and there you have it.

As I stated earlier, gozzers are very much a summer bait, but then the bream tends to be a species of fish which feeds much more freely in the warmer weather, so the need for gozzers during the winter is limited.

Casters

Since they were first used by the northern match anglers on the Trent in the late 1960s, casters, which are maggot chrysalises, have become one of the most consistently successful baits around. Every species of coarse fish seems to be vulnerable to a fresh caster, which enjoys the unique distinction of being the only living bait which does not move. Like the maggot, the caster will catch fish throughout the season, but it must be fresh. Casters quickly sour and float, and this can happen in the space of a few hours in high summer. Apart from being a killing bait for big roach and chub, they have now become the accepted feed to use in conjunction with groundbait, when fishing for bream. Many anglers turn their own casters, but I find it more economical to buy mine from the tackle shop. The wastage, unless you are turning large quantities, is substantial and the cost quite high. If you are fishing casters always give them time. They do tend to be a slow build-up bait, but once the fish move on to them they seem to like them.

Pinkies

Pink in colour, the pinkie is a small soft maggot, used mostly by canal anglers. Although I have caught good-quality fish on them from time to time, they are, in the main, only successful when smaller fish are the quarry - hence their success on canals.

Squatts

The squatt is a very small maggot, usually used as a feeder, rather than as a hook maggot. They are occasionally used as hookbait in conjunction with tiny 22 or 24 hooks by match anglers, usually when the fishing is hard in the winter.

Worms

Worms, which are a grossly underrated bait, will account for fish even in the worst conditions. They are possibly the best-known bait for bream, particularly red worms and lobworms.

Bronze pinkies.

Worms, a most underrated bait.

Brandlings are popular but they tend to die very quickly. Like maggots, worms can be used all the year round.

Hemp

Used cooked, we do not know why fish, especially roach, should like hemp, but like it they do. It is used mainly as a feed. Particularly in the summer months, roach will sometimes take it on the hook and when they do, the action is often fast and furious. It is, however, a problem bait, being difficult to keep on the hook. On such occasions tares are a better hookbait.

Tares

Tares, a kind of pea, used in conjunction with

hemp, can be a devastating hookbait during the warm summer months; but be warned, it is only a summer bait. I have known many anglers waste a lot of time trying to catch on tares in September and October. I can offer no explanation why certain baits, such as tares, only work at certain times of the year; suffice it to say such a situation does exist. Unlike casters, if you are going to catch on tares you can expect to get a bite fairly quickly. If you have not had a bite after half an hour, it is unlikely that you are going to catch anything on them.

Bread

Like worms, bread is a most underrated bait and has possibly accounted for more specimen fish than any other bait. Used as either flake or

Sweetcorn.

paste, it tends to work better in clear low water conditions. It can be used all the year round.

Sweetcorn

This is the most devastating bait for specimen fish to have appeared on the angling scene in recent years. Sweetcorn used directly from the tin will sort out the better quality-fish, including 20 lb (9 kg) plus carp, 10 lb (4.50 kg) bream and 2 lb (900 g) roach. Apart from match anglers who are always loathe to try new baits, both pleasure anglers and specimen hunters have benefited from this bait, especially on waters where the bait has been used for some time. Loose fed, like maggots, two grains of corn on a size 10 hook is a killing method. It is most effective in the summer and autumn.

Wasp grub

The largest single problem with wasp grub is acquiring it, but once acquired, it can be a killing bait for chub. It is banned on many waters in the West Midlands, because of its effectiveness. The traditional method of fishing wasp grub is to extract the grubs themselves (they look like very large white maggots). They are very soft, and although they can be made to stay on the hook, many anglers boil them for a couple of minutes before using them. This tends to make them firmer and easier to use. The remains of the cake are then broken up and mixed with groundbait. Another successful method is to fish with the cake on a size 6 or 8 hook. Like tares, wasp grub has its days. I have fished with the grub on the chub-infested

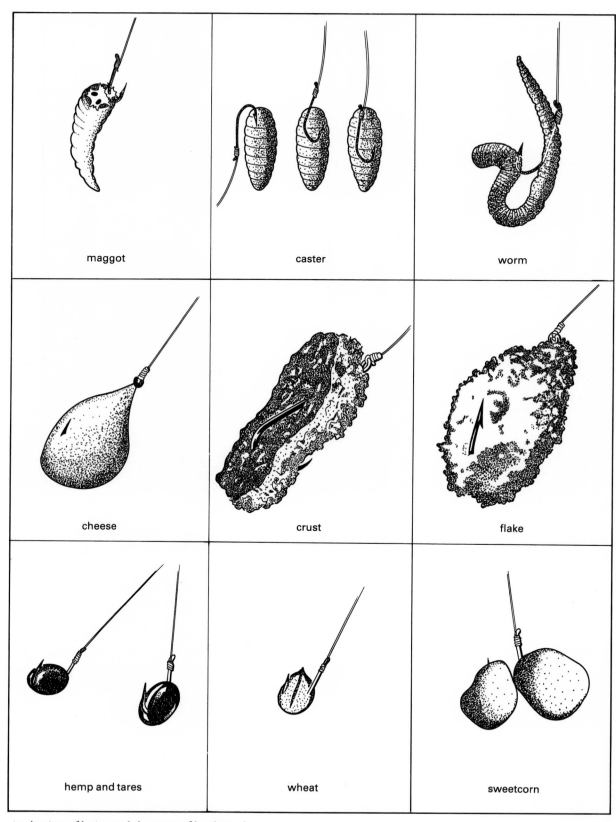

maggot

caster

worm

cheese

crust

flake

hemp and tares

wheat

sweetcorn

A selection of baits and the ways of hooking them.

Wasp grub.

Thames at Oxford without ever getting a bite, while anglers around me have caught fish after fish on the caster. Conversely, on the days when the fish are taking it, it is an arm-aching business.

Wheat

This is another summer bait, which should be cooked until it swells and softens. Wheat tends to be at its most effective during July and August. It will account for most species but is generally considered to be a roach bait. I have never caught many fish on this bait, but I know several anglers who have. It is very much a pleasure angler's bait and seldom produces in matches.

8
FEEDING

Jim Heaps, the great Stockport angler and father of former world champion Ian, once said to me, 'David, if you want to catch a lot of fish, you must feed them'. That simple piece of advice was, in retrospect, one of the most useful pieces of information I have ever been given. In fact, all I could add to Jim's statement is to say, 'Feed them, but do not fill them'.

It is possibly in the area of feeding that the contrast between the match angler and the novice is most marked. The matchman likes to build his swim slowly, developing it and extracting the maximum amount of fish in his allotted time; increasing and decreasing his rate of feed as fish move in and out of his swim. The novice sits down, throws some maggots, sometimes a handful, sometimes two handfuls, then stops. Often he will enjoy a flurry of fish, but seldom the consistent catches enjoyed by the more experienced angler.

Feeding, more than any other skill, needs to be mastered if an angler is to put together a large net of fish. He must keep the fish feeding to be in command, because when the fish stop feeding, he will stop catching.

There are two methods of feeding a swim; either by introducing loose feed by hand or catapult, or by groundbaiting. On the right day, either method can be devastating.

Loose feed

Traditionally our loose feed will be hookbait samples, as is the case when we are maggot fishing. However, it is not unusual to fish with a different bait on the hook to that loose fed into the swim, as in the case of hemp and tares or hemp and caster. What we feed is not, in my opinion, as important as when and how much. Provided that I am fishing a swim that can be reached by either throwing or catapulting my loose feed, then I will opt for this method every time. Groundbait is fine, but if I can manage without using it, I will; but more of that later. There are very few hard and fast rules in angling, but to my mind the golden rule is, 'always assume that there are fish in your swim'. You must do this, or you are in trouble because you cannot feed invisible fish.

In a match, where the approximate winning weight is generally known before the start, it is quite easy to decide on a feeding plan, because each angler has a target in mind at the beginning; if the match is going to be won with 10 lb (4.50 kg) of fish, every angler will start feeding with that weight in mind. Obviously not everybody is going to catch 10 lb (4.50 kg) so, as the match develops and the anglers realize that they have not drawn a winning peg, they will cut back their feed and fish for a lower weight in the hope of getting the lower prizes. The situation is different for the pleasure angler because he often does not know the maximum potential of his swim so he has to decide what weight he is fishing for. Few anglers are likely to catch 40 lb (18 kg) of roach with only 1 pt (0.5 litre) of maggots, but 4 pt (2.25 litres) of maggots thrown in indiscriminately will do nothing to improve the angler's chances of catching in a swim with a potential of only 3-4 lb (1.30-1.80 kg) of fish. So a decision has to be made.

Assuming that an angler decides to float fish

The author nets a 4-lb (1.8-kg) bream. On this occasion he had to wait one-and-a-half hours for his first bite but he had fed enough to enable him to catch another five without feeding again.

Above: *Maureen Richardson unhooks a 5-lb (2.2-kg) bream taken from a prebaited swim.*
Opposite: *Five match anglers with a combined catch of over 200 lb (90 kg). The result of careful feeding.*

a swim that he thinks is capable of producing 10 lb (4.50 kg) of roach, this will probably represent, allowing for the odd 8 oz (225 g) fish, approximately thirty fish. The average fishing session lasts five hours, which represents a catch rate of only six fish per hour; not a difficult task, but it can be if the angler throws in a couple of handfuls of maggots at the start. On average, the experts claim that a top-class angler will catch 10 per cent of the fish in front of him. Assuming that to be correct, what the angler hopes to do is to excite the fish into feeding by making them compete for his loose offerings. The secret is, not to throw in too much feed because this creates a situation whereby the fish can feed at their leisure. If the angler starts by feeding twenty or thirty maggots every cast, he should start to get bites pretty quickly provided that his hookbait is being presented well. The secret now is to keep the bites coming.

What many anglers fail to realize is that throughout the day there will be a turnover of fish in their swim. They might start off catching roach in the 2-3 oz (55-85 g) class, then the swim will die. They may then catch fish in the 4-6 oz (115-170 g) class. What happens is that when a shoal of better fish move into your swim, the smaller fish move out. What the angler must be prepared to do is to adjust both his

hook presentation and his feeding pattern when this happens.

It is an acknowledged fact that it is more difficult to fish efficiently in rivers than on stillwaters, but, in the area of feeding, the situation is reversed. The river angler can overfeed his swim, but because that feed is being carried away by the current, no lasting harm is done, unless of course he continues to overfeed. The stillwater angler does not enjoy such an advantage. Whatever feed he puts in stays on the bottom. Consequently, if he has fed in 200 maggots at the start and there are only 100 fish in front of him, it is going to be pure good fortune if one of the fish picks up his hookbait. Furthermore, because of the abundance of food which is now lying on the bottom, a number of fish will become well fed within a short space of time and instead of having 100 feeding fish in front of him the angler could, within the space of ten or fifteen minutes, have reduced this to sixty or even less. By introducing another large handful of maggots this number can quickly be reduced even further and rather than developing the swim, slowly building it up, so that the maximum number of fish can be caught, the swim will have been destroyed by indiscriminate feeding.

Always start slowly, introducing only ten to twenty maggots at a time. If the fish are there,

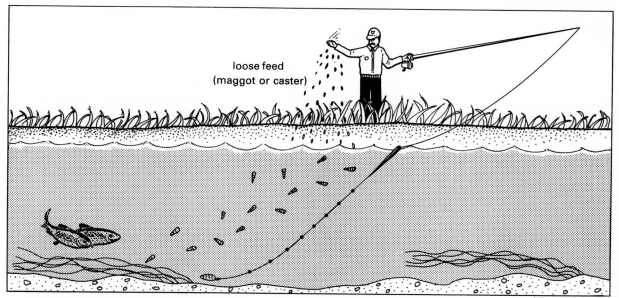

Loose feed, such as maggot or caster, being thrown in by hand.

you will begin to get bites. The secret is to feed every cast, so that your hookbait is falling through the water with your loose feed. If you find that the fish are coming off the bottom and taking your bait 'on the drop', adjust your shotting accordingly. However, if you find that only the smaller fish are coming up in the water while the better fish continue feeding on the bottom, step up your feed, because much of what you are putting in is not reaching the bottom, it is being intercepted by the smaller fish in midwater. If you do not get food to the better fish, they will move, especially if they are in the mood to feed.

I think that a point needs to be made here concerning small fish feeding in midwater. When you find yourself in this situation and you are fishing for the bigger fish on the bottom, if on the way down your float dips but a proper bite does not manifest itself, always reel in and check your maggot; nine times out of ten you will find the end nipped. You will seldom get a bite once your maggot has burst, so there seems little point in sitting ten minutes waiting for a bite which is not going to come, when it takes only seconds to change a maggot and recast.

One has read many times that the best method of loose feeding is 'little and often', but it is an ambiguous statement. 'A little and often'

on fast-flowing rivers like the Trent or the Severn constitutes throwing in much more feed than on a stillwater or a canal, simply because you are casting and feeding more often. To be more precise, I would suggest that you feed for one fish at a time, once you have caught it, fish for your next one. By doing this, you will not make the mistake of throwing feed in indiscriminately, a root cause of many spoilt swims.

Groundbait

I stated earlier that whenever possible I prefer loose feed to groundbait. I said this for a number of reasons, but mainly because I am never sure how the fish in my swim will react to the introduction of cereal. Groundbait can - and often does - kill a swim completely, even when introduced by an expert like Ivan Marks. On the other hand, it can also bring a flagging swim back to life.

Let us start at the beginning, by defining exactly what good groundbait is, because much of what is sold in tackle shops is anything but good. The best groundbait is finely ground breadcrumb, not biscuit or rusk, just plain bread. When mixed it should be fluffy, not stodgy, and it should cloud as it strikes the surface of the water. I do not use any groundbaits mixed with additives like meat or fish because

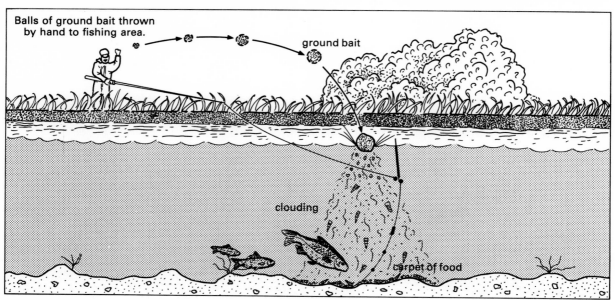

Groundbait clouding and providing a carpet of food on the bottom.

A tennis-ball-sized ball of groundbait laced with casters.

A ball of groundbait broken open, showing the amount of feed each ball should contain.

in my opinion they do not fulfil the function I want my groundbait to perform.

Principally, I use groundbait under the following circumstances: if I am fishing at distance, beyond the range of my loose feed catapult; and almost always when I am fishing for bream. There are other occasions, of course, such as on deep rivers, but generally I associate groundbait with bream. What many novice anglers fail to realize is that groundbait is used by the experienced angler as a carrier and not as a feed. I am surprised at the number of occasions when I have witnessed anglers simply throwing in groundbait. All they are doing is throwing money away.

We do not know why bream respond so well to groundbait, but of all the coarse fish bream is the one species that responds best to this method of feeding. Although they can be caught with loose feed, they are by nature nervous fish, seldom caught close in, but, preferring to roam 33-44 yd (30-40 m) from the bank. Because bream are nervous, feeding correctly is crucial. I have often seen a shoal of bream feeding quite happily, then one wrong move and they are gone. The most difficult situation you can encounter when bream fishing, is to start fishing with the shoal already in front of you. Do you feed and possibly frighten them away, or fish without feeding, in which case they will drift away, possibly to the next angler on the bank? In all honesty there is no answer to that one. What I do is mix my groundbait as wet as possible so that it goes in with the minimum amount of disturbance. If they move, I have done the wrong thing, if they stay I have won the match.

Accepting that groundbait in itself is not adequate feed to stop a patrolling shoal of bream, what we want is a mixture of feed and groundbait that, upon impact with the water, will cloud and fall to the bottom to create a carpet of feed, which will prove attractive to the fish. What we do not want is a series of little mounds, which is what happens when groundbait is incorrectly mixed. The correct utensil for mixing groundbait is a shallow wide-topped bowl, not a bucket, which I see many anglers using. How often have you seen anglers adding water to a

bucket of groundbait? The outcome is wet, sloppy groundbait on the top and dry groundbait on the bottom. Always put the water in the bowl first then add the groundbait, the reason for this is that by adding the groundbait to the water you ensure that it is all dampened evenly. Having done that, you should have a nice fluffy texture, not a stodgy mess. Now add your feed. As a rule of thumb, I add 1 pt (500 ml) of casters or squatts to every pound of groundbait. That may sound a lot, but because groundbait is inexpensive compared to casters or maggots, anglers invariably mix too much groundbait. I never mix maggots with my groundbait, firstly because they can break up the ball in the air, and secondly, as it is possible to wait for up to an hour for a bite, I never feel confident that they will remain lying on top of my groundbait, whereas casters do not move.

Try, if you can, to imagine a plate of curry served on a bed of rice; the whole thing is most appetizing, especially the tasty pieces of succulent meat nestling amid the sauce. The rice, apart from setting the scene, offers little in the way of real taste; it is stodge. Now mix up the whole thing and suddenly the rice is as tasty as the rest of the meal, so rather than discriminate as we might have done whilst the dish was well set out, we now tuck in indiscriminately. What has this to do with fishing, you might ask? If you have mixed your groundbait properly, so that it breaks into a cloud upon contact with the water, the effect when it reaches the bottom will be of casters nestling on a fine bed of groundbait. If, on the other hand, you have, like so many anglers, mixed a bowl of stodgy groundbait, the outcome will be that the ball will not break up until it reaches the bed of the lake or river, and will leave little lumps of feed here and there, like the curry and rice when mixed. Instead of the casters alone being totally irresistible, the stodge with casters embedded becomes attractive to the fish. If your caster hookbait is nearby it will probably be taken by the fish, but we are filling the fish up with stodge at the same time, which we do not want

Over 200 lb (90 kg) of tench and bream caught in Ireland by Sheffield's Pete Evans and Dave Piddington.

to do. Remember what I said at the beginning of this chapter, we want to 'feed them, but not fill them'.

Except when I find a shoal of fish in front of me, I like, if possible, to get my feed in before the bream move into my swim, I do not like to put feed on top of a shoal of feeding bream. Sometimes we have to, and they do not always seem to mind, but it is the exception rather than the rule. Having chosen my swim I will generally open up with three balls the size of tennis balls, laced with either squatts or casters. From then on, my feeding is dependent upon two things: what I hope to catch, and where the fish are. If I am only expecting to catch two or three fish, I will possibly add another two balls at the off and leave it at that. If I am hoping to put a weight together, then after my initial three balls, I will do nothing for fifteen minutes, other than watch for signs, line bites and so on. If I get no signs then I will proceed to feed at regular intervals, until either I see indications of fish being there or the anglers on either side of me catch a bream. By that time I am hopeful that I have enough feed in my swim to hold them.

Baits change; at the time of writing loose-fed bronze maggots are dominating the match fishing scene, but it is the way in which they are fed that accounts for their success. There are no secret baits and no secret feeding patterns. Master this aspect of fishing and you will be well on your way to becoming the complete coarse fisherman.

9
CANAL FISHING

It is unusual to find an angler who has not fished a canal at some time in his life, for canals have been the training ground for many of today's top anglers. And although very few canals support a head of large fish, canal fishing really can be fun.

The secret of success on canals is to think small; ½ pt (250 ml) of pinkies is generally plenty of bait for a session. Remember that whatever you put in cannot be taken out. I say this because I have lost count of the number of anglers I have seen kill their swim on a canal before they have even started to fish. The old adage of 'fish for a fish, and when you have caught that one, fish for another,' is certainly sound advice as far as most canals are concerned. Of course, not all canals are alike. Some, like the Gloucester canal, are wide and deep, carrying all manner of sea-going vessels. This type of canal is a law unto itself. The type of canal I intend to write about is the type which was built during the last century: the Grand Union, the Leeds-Liverpool; purpose-built for the horse-drawn barge industry. On most canals, the horse-drawn barge is long gone, replaced by the pleasure craft which abound during the summer months and play an important part in the way in which we approach canal fishing.

If you are fortunate enough to live by a canal which is not infested with boat traffic, then you are the lucky one, for most canal anglers have now come to accept the boats. In fact in many respects, the boats dictate where the fish live. On clear boat-free canals most fish are caught in the deeper water found in the middle of the canal, but anybody who has witnessed the churning mud created by a pleasure cruiser will quickly understand why this is not the case on the canals which support boats. For this reason, before we start fishing it is crucial that we locate the shelves which exist on every canal, for it is here that the fish are to be found.

The roach disease in the 1960s hit canal fishing very hard. Consequently, for a number of years the canals in the northwest and the Midlands did not receive the attention they deserved. But with the return of roach to these waters, we have witnessed a revival of canal fishing and with it, an upturn in standards. Anglers like Billy Makin, Mick Hiatt, Ray Mills and the northern anglers, Harry Settle, Dave Roper and Dave Brogden, appear to be able to catch fish wherever they are drawn.

In match fishing terms, there are two types of canals: those that are dominated by bloodworm and those that are not. In the northwest, canals, like the Lancaster canal, are totally dominated by bloodworm, or 'little red men' as they are known; other baits are not used. However, in the south and the Midlands, whilst bloodworm account for a lot of fish, the scope is much greater, with bread-punch, pinkies, squatts, maggots and casters all proving to be just as effective.

Feeding

In the full knowledge that whatever bait we put in stays in, the initial approach, having established the whereabouts of the shelves, is one of caution. Accepting that boat traffic will dis-

rupt the centre of the canal, we generally have four options open to us: the top of the nearside shelf, where we can expect to find gudgeon, and the odd small roach (1 oz/30 g); the bottom of the nearside shelf, invariably a holding place for roach in the 1-3 oz (30-85 g) class; the bottom of the far shelf, where small roach and gudgeon are found; and the top far side shelf, where we find the quality roach and skimmers. Obviously it is impossible to be specific. For example, if a canal is gin clear, you are not likely to find 4-5 oz (115-140 g) roach on top of a 2 ft (60 cm) shelf, but on most canals where boat traffic causes the water to be coloured, it is quite normal to find the quality fish lying in 2 ft (60 cm) of water. In fact, during the winter of 1978, I caught a perch weighing 1 lb 7 oz (650 g) in only 12 in (30 cm) of water.

In recent years one of the most productive baits I have used on canals is bread punch. The great beauty of this bait is that it is instant; if you are going to catch with it, a bite will be registered within five minutes. Fished in conjunction with tiny thumbnail-sized balls of cloud groundbait, it can be devastating on a canal which has been allowed to settle overnight. The problem is that almost immediately the first boat has passed, stirring up the mud, a decline in bites occurs and a change to the pinkie is signalled. Caster can be devasting, but it is a slow build-up bait; normally I tend to start fishing at the bottom of the nearside shelf and loose feed casters on to the top of the far shelf, giving the fish at least thirty minutes to find them before I go over with a single caster buried in a size 20 fine wire hook. Like the bread punch, the caster is often a fairly instant success, provided that you have given the fish time to find them.

Tackle

Tackle for canal fishing needs to be light. I can think of no reason why, on a water where a fish weighing over 8 oz (225 g) is the exception rather than the rule, anglers should want to fish

The author fishing the Grand Union Canal for roach and skimmer bream at Muscott Mill near Daventry.

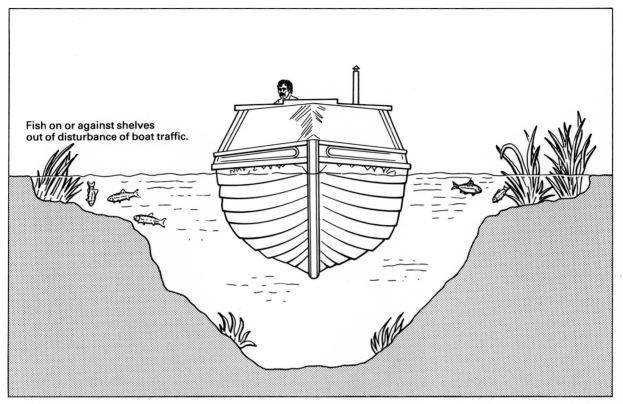

A canal profile showing boat traffic and shoals of fish.

with 3 lb (1.35 kg) or even 2 lb (0.90 kg) line. I use a 1.7 lb (0.77 g) reel line and 1.1 lb (0.50 kg) hook length. I cannot ever remember having my line broken. I keep shotting to a minimum. Remember you are only fishing 2 ft (60 cm) deep, and even in the boat channel it is unlikely that you will find more than 6 ft (1.80 m), so the need for a lot of shot on the line is eliminated. I tend to place all of my shot around the float with either a single No. 8 or No.10 shot 9 in (22 cm) from the hook. Floats are a question of personal choice. I usually use the continental type with a bristle for fishing the near-

side and the Ultra type canal dart for the far bank.

I once had a good tip from that great canal angler Mick Hiatt: when you hook a good fish on a canal, always play it deep and try to keep the amount of splashing on the surface to a minimum because it doesn't take much to frighten a shoal of fish in 2 ft (60 cm) of water.

Treat the canal with respect and you will catch a lot of fish; make a noise or overfeed and you will sit biteless for hours.

10
POLE FISHING

Not many seasons ago, the angler seen using a pole was often the target for jokes and laughter. Now, however, the smiles have faded and the jokes come less often, because during the past few years there has been something of a pole revolution in this country, particularly among the match angling fraternity.

It is inevitable that the pole will eventually find its way into every match angler's holdall, and that many pleasure anglers will come to appreciate its use; inevitable, because it is a fact that in the right conditions the pole is unbeatable.

When it comes to catching small fish at close range, the pole is often far superior to our traditional rod and line. With the addition of the elastic shock absorber it becomes an even more versatile weapon. Fish up to 2 lb (900 g) can also be successfully dealt with. It is only when the need arises to fish further out from the bank than, say, 30 ft (9 m) or long trot, that our normal running line tackle comes into its own. The angler who is conversant with both the pole and traditional running line tackle is the best equipped of all.

There are two types of pole, the softer telescopic and the more rigid take-apart.

The telescopic pole

The telescopic pole is less commonly used. It has a soft action all through and the line is tied direct to the tip. This type of pole is ideal when small fish are encountered in quantity, particularly on the surface or in shallow water, and it is ideal for fishing at speed. The ideal material,

naturally enough, is fibreglass. The reason a soft action is required is that when fishing at speed, especially for bleak, there is a lot less effort required in casting with this type of pole. Also, and again especially with bleak, the soft action prevents the fish being pulled off the hook when you strike.

The take-apart pole

The more common and versatile pole is the take-apart type, built to hold a metal crook and elastic shock absorber or a flick tip, depending on the type of fishing you are doing.

What should you look for when buying this type of pole? There are two main points: rigidity and lightness. Fibreglass is the ideal material for the latter consideration. The best poles combine the two qualities to produce the right medium, for unlike the traditional fishing rod which has to be soft actioned for both casting and striking, this is not the case with a pole. Tackle is simply swung out, and the elastic cushions the strike, so the pole can be made rigid and more manageable.

On the continent, an angler will have a range of three or more poles, varying in length between 6½-30 ft (2-10 m); even in this country a range of poles is required on many waters. For the beginner though, I would suggest a single pole of 20 ft (6 m) in length. Many anglers seem to forget that because the pole can be fished in sections, it makes sense to purchase the longest pole you can afford. It is easy to fish with 10 ft (3 m) of a 20 ft (6 m) pole but impossible to fish 20 ft (6 m) if your pole is only 10 ft

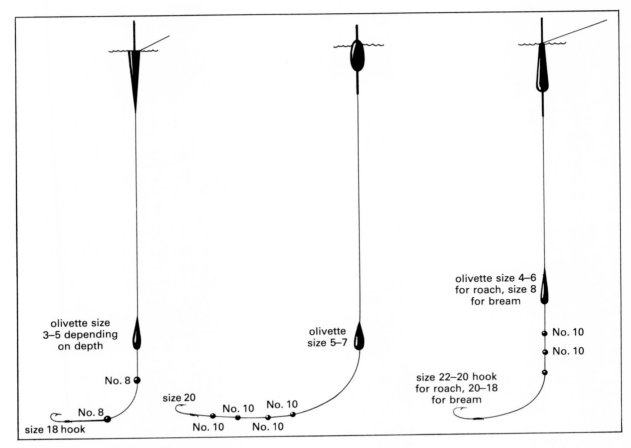

The basic terminal pole tackle.

olivette size
3–5 depending
on depth

No. 8

No. 8

size 18 hook

size 20

No. 10   No. 10

No. 10   No. 10

olivette
size 5–7

olivette size 4–6
for roach, size 8
for bream

No. 10

No. 10

size 22–20 hook
for roach, 20–18
for bream

(3 m) long.

The biggest mistake many newcomers to pole fishing make is that they often have far too much line between pole tip and float, thus defeating the pole's great advantage: superior control over tackle. When using the type of rigid pole just described, the nearer your float is to the tip of the pole, the better. Ideally, the float should be no more than 3 ft (1 m) from the pole tip, so that whatever the conditions you have maximum control over your tackle. It is this ability to control your tackle so perfectly, and thus present your bait in the most natural manner, that is the superior advantage of the pole.

The flick tip

This looks rather like a long quivertip; it has the line tied directly to it and is used for small fish. This is the ideal sort of pole to use when blood-worm fishing, unless you expect to catch fish over, say, 4 oz (115 g).

The crook

The alloy crook and elastic shock absorber need to be explained in more depth because, correctly used, these items of tackle absolutely paralyse fish and give you an advantage that no item of British tackle can.

The alloy crook is fitted to the top of your pole where it 'crooks' downwards between the pole and the terminal tackle. It is designed to hold the elastic shock absorber and is either a part of the pole when you buy it, or can be purchased separately afterwards.

The purpose of the crook is twofold. Firstly, it minimizes the possibility of tangles; and secondly, it enables you to change your tackle at

The author effectively using a pole for lake fishing.

Top match angler, Joe Brennan, using a pole to swing in a roach on Ulster's River Bann.

will. The elastic is fitted at the end of your crook. It is attached by slotting a loop of elastic into the slit at the end of the crook, and it is held in place by sliding a fitted piece of plastic tubing down over the loop.

The elastic comes in four strengths, and will stretch to five or six times its own length. Over the counter, it is sold in pre-wound lengths and is cut to the required length by the angler at home.

The main advantage of the elastic is that it enables you to use delicate terminal tackle. A continental angler will often be using the elastic in conjunction with line of 8 oz (2.25 g) breaking strain; the hook itself may be as small as 26. The elastic absorbs any initial pull, whenever a decent-sized fish is hooked and therefore protects the fragile tackle.

Let me ask what would happen to such light terminal tackle if it were not backed up by the elastic? Easy! Goodbye fish!

Yet another advantage of the elastic is evident when a fish pulls the elastic under tension. The further the fish travels from the pole, the stronger the tension becomes. Eventually the fish follows the line of least resistance, giving in to the tension applied by the elastic. If large fish are to be landed with the pole and light tackle,

the elastic shock absorber is a necessity.

Terminal rigs

The exact pole rig to use with your alloy crook and flick tip obviously depends on conditions on the day, the venue and so on. However, these rigs are generally made up at home by the individual angler and kept on plastic pole winders, always ready to be looped on to the crook or flick tip when conditions demand. In fact, many continental anglers carry as many as 300 such winders around with them. One of the main reasons for this is that it is difficult to make up such tackle on the bank. Because of the delicate nature of the floats one is able to use when pole fishing, they require very careful shotting, often with tiny shot - a task that is difficult enough on the kitchen table at home!

The pole, unlike most items of tackle carried by the British angler, is something that still has to be put into true perspective by many anglers, myself included. At the start of a match I still often think, 'Would it be worth using a pole today?' Only experience can answer that question, but one thing is certain: the pole is here to stay.

11
PIKE FISHING

Of all the fish in our lakes and rivers, pike are without doubt the most abused. Many is the time I have seen anglers having enjoyed first-class sport with a pike of 6-7 lb (3-3.10 kg), throw it up the bank to die a slow, lingering death, instead of returning it to the water. That this situation exists appals me, because it is ignorance on the part of many anglers that leads them to believe, quite wrongly, that pike destroy fisheries. In fact, with few exceptions, the opposite is true. Pike, like all predators, retain a balance within their environment. Lions do not endeavour to eat every zebra, nor do they waste their energy trying to catch the fittest animal in the herd, they feed on the old and infirm animals and then only when they are hungry. Exactly the same situation exists with pike. More important is the fact that fish, unlike mammals, cannot leave behind a diseased member of the shoal, particularly in stillwaters, and this is where pike play a major part in keeping disease among fish to a minimum. Without these predators, it is possible for a whole fishery to be wiped out by a single disease.

Many anglers assume that pike swim around with their mouths open, mopping up roach and bream rather like a vacuum cleaner. In fact, pike feed for short periods only each day, perhaps for only one hour, and having fed, they are satisfied. That pike will take a dead bait is evidence that they eat dead fish. It is not unreasonable to assume that in a mixed fishery holding as many as 100,000 fish, there is a number of fish dying of natural causes at any one time. These fish obviously contribute greatly to a pike's staple diet. Why anglers should assume

that fish never die of old age is totally beyond my comprehension. The fact is, that anglers choose to believe the worst of pike.

There is, however, a growing band of pike anglers who are quite rightly concerned about the conservation of the species, their slogan being, 'Put Pike Back'. The reformed Pike Angler's Club, run by those three excellent anglers, Dr Barrie Rickards, Hugh Reynolds and Bill Chillingsworth, are doing much to educate those anglers who, because of their inexperience, are responsible for deep-hooked pike, the cause of the slow, lingering death of many fish.

Tackle

Many pleasure anglers will, during the course of a session, set up a rod using a shop-bought Fishing Gazette type pike float, fix a couple of trebles into a live bait and cast it out, leaving it to fish for itself. They then carry on fishing for roach or whatever, and sometime later they notice that the pike float has either disappeared or is being towed across the surface. Invariably by this time the damage is done. The hooks are deep into the pike's throat and unless the angler knows exactly how to deal with this situation, and owns a good pair of artery forceps, the fish is as good as dead.

However, this situation need not exist. If you are going to take up pike fishing, make sure you are properly equipped. A good pike rod is essential; a discarded 6 ft (1.85 m) boat rod is not the answer. As with match rods, the advent of fibreglass has meant that there is now a good

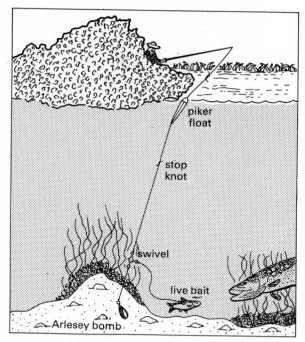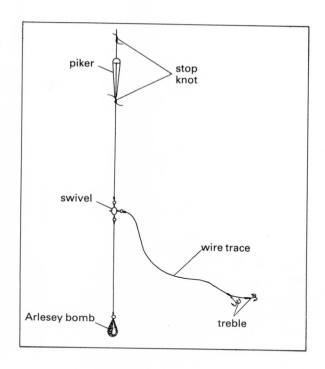

Fishing for pike and the basic pike set-up.

selection of pike rods on the market. Terry Eustace, Trevor Moss, Allan Brown and Going Bros., all make high-quality specialist rods and floats. The Fishing Gazette float is adequate but Trevor Moss of Gainsborough sells a range which will do the job much more efficiently. You do not need an enormous bung to hold up a 2 oz (55 g) roach, and the same applies to trebles. Time and time again I have seen anglers using barbed trebles, which are much too large for the baits they are using. Many of today's top pike anglers are using size 12 and 14 trebles with only the hook which is inserted into the bait barbed. The barbs on the other two hooks are either snipped off or flattened. This obviously makes unhooking the fish that much easier. Shop-bought trebles and traces are all right, but invariably the hooks are too big and too close together, and the traces are too thick. As with all fishing, the thinking angler catches the most fish. There is no point in using size 6 trebles and 30 lb (14 kg) wire traces if a size 12 treble and 18 lb (8.10 kg) wire traces will do the job better.

The problem is that the angler who buys his trebles and traces from the local tackle shop is invariably inexperienced. He ties his line directly to the wire trace. When he gets a run and it is put under pressure, the wire trace often cuts through the monofilament line, causing a breakage. The pike escapes and is left to gorge the bait, complete with trebles. This could be overcome quite simply by using a swivel to join the wire and the nylon. If anglers could be persuaded to make up their own traces they would in fact be fishing with a better product. Treble hooks can be bought in a selection of sizes from most good tackle shops, and Sea Strand trolling wire and Marlin steel wire are available from most specialist shops. These are both excellent multi-strand wires. There was a move some time ago to single-strand wire, but unfortunately this type of wire kinks and when it does so, it can be broken like cotton. Because it has this weakness, I never use single-strand wire.

Baiting the hook

When it comes to mounting a bait, the secret is to mount it in such a position that however the pike takes it, either one or both trebles will be in its mouth. Always remember that a deep-hooked pike is a dead pike, so we want to be

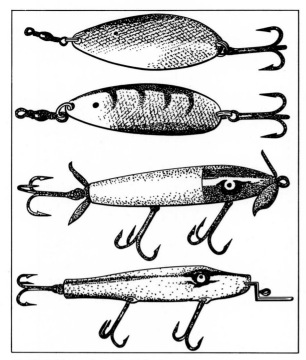

Artificial lures for pike fishing.

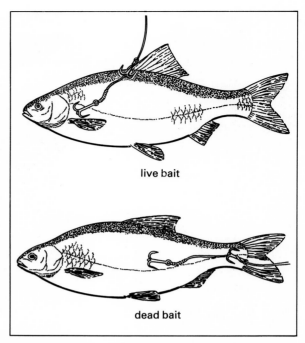

The correct method of baiting the hooks with live bait and with dead bait.

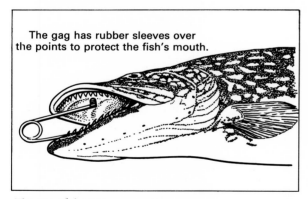

The use of the gag.

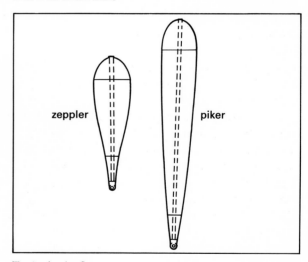

Typical pike floats.

sure that the hooks are in the mouth, not the throat. Most people will have read or been told that when a run occurs, they should count to ten and then strike. I have even read a book in which the riter has described smoking a cigarette whilst the pike towed his bait around. This is all nonsense. When your float goes under or starts to move, then your bait and hook, if it is mounted properly, are in the pike's mouth so strike immediately. You might lose the odd

Previous page: *Over 20 lb (9 kg) of hard-fighting pike, our largest predatory fish.*

fish, but you are not going to kill any. *Always strike immediately a run occurs.*

When you are using a small live bait, and by that I mean a 1-2 oz (30-55 g) fish, it is not necessary to use two trebles; one semi-barbless treble set into the dorsal fin will do the job. Any pike, even one of 3 lb (1.30 kg), will take a bait of this size straight into its mouth. If I am using a larger bait, I place a treble under the dorsal fin which takes the impact of the cast and the sec-

Barry Burton plays a large Fenland pike.

ond in the muscle surrounding the pectoral fin. John Watson of Blackpool - possibly one of today's leading pike anglers - shares my opinion that many anglers place their trebles too far apart. When fishing with dead baits, one treble will generally be inserted in the tail root so it is asking for trouble to place the second in the head or the gill cover, the pike takes the bait head first and the hooks must go down its throat. Always try to keep the hooks as far back as possible.

There has been some conjecture in recent years that if a deeply hooked pike is returned to the water with the hooks still in its throat, its natural juices will in some way dissolve the hook. Where this theory comes from I do not know, but I cannot subscribe to it. I do not believe that anything happens other than that the pike dies a slow and agonizing death. If you catch a pike and you cannot get the hooks out, kill it quickly and painlessly. However, the answer is, not to deep-hook them in the first place.

Young anglers often fish for pike and then,

Pete Evans lands a Loch Lomond pike.

Mick Brown poses with a 17 lb 12 oz (7.9-kg) specimen.

having caught one, are terrified to go near it. This is foolishness. Once a pike is on the bank he is in no mood for a fight; he is dying. Ask yourself, if you were drowning, would you be looking to stay in the water? Of course not. All the pike wants to do is to get back into the water, so get those hooks out and put him back. Never use a gaff; fortunately we do not see this disgusting practice much these days, but the time was when anglers did use them and what a terrible mess they used to make.

Pike fishing can be exciting but always try to remember that future generations will only be able to enjoy good fishing if we conserve our fisheries.

Live baits or dead baits?

I am often asked by anglers whether it is morally right to fish with live baits, when dead baits are so effective, as are plugs and spinners. The answer is, that it is a matter for each man's conscience. I never use live baits these days, but having said that, I know that live baits account for many fish.

Dr Barrie Rickards and Ray Webb, in their book on pike fishing, stated that at certain times, dead baits were the most effective bait, whilst on other occasions they were unable to get a bite on a dead bait and yet in the same swim a live bait would be snapped up immediately. Much in the same way as on occasions bream will not take a float-fished maggot, but will take the bait if it is legered.

There is much we do not know about fish. Why in the summer will pike take a spinner, which in no way resembles a fish? Why do they feed for short periods, often at the same time each day, then suddenly a change of wind direction will find them feeding at a different time? Why do 'hot spots' exist? If you are to become a successful pike angler, as in other branches of the sport, there is much to learn, but once learned the action can be most exciting. There can be few greater experiences than returning your first 20 lb (9 kg) pike back to the water - alive.

12
MATCH FISHING

There is evidence to suggest that the boom in angling witnessed during the 1950s has now settled down and in fact slightly fewer people are now going fishing than ten years ago. However, one area of angling that is still growing is match fishing.

Unlike other sports, there are no professional match anglers. By that I mean that no one earns his living by fishing in competitions. With so few really large sponsored events, it is impossible to earn a living wage, but as the match fishing side of the sport develops and more and more of the larger companies invest a proportion of their profits in sports sponsorship, it is possible that in the next decade we could see a number of professional anglers beginning to emerge.

It has often been suggested that match anglers are primarily motivated by greed, by the desire to profit from their chosen sport. In reality this is far from the truth, for whilst match winnings are always gratefully accepted - particularly now, with the cost of fishing in a match being anything from £10 to £15 - it is the spirit of competition that appeals to most match anglers.

Because there are no professional anglers, there is no professional match circuit. Any member of the public can buy a ticket for a match and find himself drawn next to ex-world champions: Ian Heaps, Robin Harris or any of the other top names. In this respect match fishing is unique, for I can think of no other sport where that situation exists. And, of course, because we cannot see our quarry, it is quite possible for an unknown angler to enjoy the

satisfaction of beating a world champion off the next peg.

Match angling is fun at all levels, from the smallest club match to the big open competitions. Because people do not rely on their match winnings to form part of their income, there is seldom the pressure that one finds in other sports.

Anglers turn to match fishing for a variety of reasons: the opportunity to fish waters not normally open to them; to fish with friends who are already match fishing; or because they feel the need to compete. As in all things, there is no easy way to the top, few men get there in match fishing without serving a lengthy apprenticeship.

The great problem with angling is that there is so much to learn. An angler can become an expert on a river like the Trent; visit a similar river, like the Severn, and find his methods do not yield a single fish. Time and time again a river responds to a particular method, with matches being won week after week by anglers employing that method. Then, seemingly overnight, that method does not work. Suddenly a new method is winning the matches; it happens constantly.

As a youth I played cricket and football. If I were to return to these sports today, very little would have changed, but not so in match angling. An angler who has not fished for twenty years could not compete today, even at club level. In fact, an angler who has been away from

Opposite: *The weigh-in!*

A pole-caught fish being brought to the net on Cheshire's River Weaver.

A match in progress on the Grand Union Canal.

the sport for only five years would have difficulty competing. The angler who achieves success in match fishing must be well informed all of the time.

Club matches

Most anglers come into match fishing by joining a club, of which there are thousands. Most clubs run a match once a fortnight during the summer and once a month during the winter. These can be anything from ten pegs to fifty pegs, and the standard in the main is not particularly high, although I should add that this is not always the case. Most club matches are staged on waters owned by other associations and the pegs are booked for the day. Consequently the club anglers, unlike open match anglers, who are well versed about most match venues, find themselves on a piece of water about which they know very little. And, because they are mostly in full-time employment, they have been unable to practise the week before. In fact, upon arrival at the bank, many of them will be seeing the water for the first time. In some respects this is the fairest way of staging a match. The good pegs and the hot spots are not known, so everybody has a more or less equal chance, and as long as the best anglers do not draw pegs which are devoid of fish, they should win the match.

Most clubs run a points system during the season. The winner of each match will be allotted, say, ten points, the second man nine points, the third eight points, and so on. At the end of the season the points are added up and the angler with the most points wins the much coveted Points Cup. This tradition exists in more or less every club and it is the cup every angler wants to win, because it is a true measure of the winner's ability to do well on a variety of waters.

Unlike open match fishing, the club angler is seldom confronted with local experts. These are the anglers who set the tremendously high standard that exists on the open match circuit. To try to define in a layman's terms the gap that exists between the club angler and the open match angler, I would have to say that it is simi-

Angling journalist, Mark Downes, winner of the 1986 Sealink Classic, Europe's most prestigious angling competition.

lar to that between fourth and first division footballers.

Open matches

As petrol and bait costs continue to rise, more and more open match anglers are concentrating on waters in the immediate vicinity of their homes. Time was, when an open match on the North Bank at Peterborough would attract anglers from as far afield as Sheffield, London, Birmingham, and Wolverhampton. A match on the Trent would attract anglers from Manchester, Newcastle, and Lincoln, but not so today. Because of inflation, the Nottingham anglers have committed themselves to mastering their local river, the Trent. Many of these anglers, such as Frank Barlow, John Rolfe, Ted Stokes, Pete Palmer, Wayne Swinscoe and John Dean are so accomplished on the river that given the luck to draw one of the the noted pegs, they are virtually unbeatable. The same situation exists on every major match water. With local anglers having access so freely to the water, they quickly adapt to any changes which may occur, such as the fish showing preference for a different bait, or a new method. However, not all open match anglers enjoy the luxury of a match water near their homes. They are forced to travel to find good matches, and they have to be very competent if they are to compete with this new breed of extremely capable local experts. Hence the high standard that now exists on the open match circuit.

How does the club angler make the transition on to the open match circuit? Having achieved consistent success at club level many anglers feel the need to move on to a bigger challenge. Until ten years ago open matches were few and far between so the club angler was able to mix the two successfully, fishing a club match each weekend and open matches as and when they were staged. Since then, the situation has changed and as many as thirty open matches are staged every Saturday. To be successful on the open match circuit now, the angler has to commit himself to fishing open matches on a regular basis. The club angler who has a good open match venue close to hand, must - if he is to be successful - take advantage of that venue. The opportunity to practise on a venue is crucial. With match costs so high, very few anglers can afford to fish matches without getting a return on their investment, and it is unlikely that the newcomers will win very much by travelling here, there and everywhere.

If a club angler does not have a match venue close by, he should analyse his strengths and weaknesses and look at the methods that have brought him success in his club matches - legering, stick float or waggler - and the type of venue on which he has been successful. He must then look for matches where he can fish the methods at which he is most adept. Confidence is everything in match fishing and confidence comes from success.

It is often thought that the top match anglers are successful because they have access to secret baits and methods. In fact, this is nonsense; there are no secrets in fishing. The top anglers are more successful because they are more dedicated and more skilful than the less successful anglers. Unlike sports where a sense of timing or balance are sufficient to make the participant a competent competitor, successful angling is the coming together of many different kinds of skills: watercraft (the ability to read a piece of water accurately), casting, feeding, float control, and patience. All of these skills need to be mastered before an angler can begin to compete. It takes years, but even then it is necessary to strive constantly for improvement. Clive Smith, former captain of one of the most successful fishing teams of all time, the BAA, is a master float angler and yet he has never won more than nine open matches in one season. Ivan Marks, the most successful post-war match angler, won eighteen matches during the 1961-62 season, but accepts that if he wins five or six opens during a season on the current match circuit he has had a successful season. Such is the competition on the open match circuit, especially when you consider that both Ivan and Clive fish in excess of sixty matches during the course of a season.

Anglers are not obliged to fish open matches; the club match scene has never been healthier than it is today. It is far less demanding and in the main, because the rewards are not so great, it can be more fun. Like most of today's open match anglers, I fished at club level for many years. I learned a lot, made many good friends and enjoyed my fishing just as much as I do today. Not all anglers strive to reach the top; they are content to fish in the company of friends, considering a win as something of a bonus. Fishing is something they do to relax; they compete, but on their own terms, and they are, none-the-less, an integral part of the match fishing scene.

13
SPECIMEN HUNTING

Eric Hodgeson, the long-serving secretary of the National Association of Specimen Groups once described specimen hunters thus: 'We are pleasure anglers who fish for big fish' - an apt description.

Most anglers take up the sport as youngsters. Some are content merely to catch a few fish from time to time, whilst others strive constantly for improvement. It is the latter who invariably find their way into match fishing or specimen hunting. It is generally considered that the top match angler is the most talented of all anglers, but in reality the top specimen hunter is no less talented. That anglers of the calibre of Kevin Clifford, Dave Plummer, John Watson and Jim Gibbinson catch big fish consistently, is evidence of this fact.

Because, in recent years, a number of extremists have sought publicity in the angling press, there is a popular misconception that specimen hunters spend their nights creeping from tree to tree in heavy disguise casting baits to unseen fish. They are supposedly secretive and often eccentric. Of course, this is nonsense. In the main, most successful specimen hunters are normal people who simply enjoy catching big fish.

All anglers, even match anglers, enjoy catching big fish, but to most people the capture of a specimen-sized fish is a bonus. The average angler sets out to catch fish, any fish, and the match angler sets out to catch the maximum number of fish: because of this, they fish with baits which are universal in appeal. The specimen hunter, on the other hand, has much more clearly defined objectives. Firstly,

he knows what species of fish he is fishing for; secondly, he selects a bait which will appeal to that fish; and thirdly, he will only fish waters which he knows for a fact hold the fish he is fishing for.

Fish location

Ask any successful specimen hunter for the secret of consistent success in the big fish world and the chances are he will tell you that it is fish location. To become a successful specimen hunter you must fish the right waters, i.e., waters that hold a head of big fish. Few waters which are full of fish ever produce big fish consistently. They do, however, from time to time produce the odd specimen, but it is the exception rather than the rule. The true speciemn hunter is prepared to sit for hours, sometimes days, in the knowledge that when a bite does materialize, the chances are that it will be a big fish.

Like match anglers, most specimen hunters start at the bottom, fishing club and day ticket waters. Without doubt, it is more difficult to catch large fish on these waters but graduating to fishing for near-record fish is a slow process. An angler does not become a specimen hunter and then immediately begin fishing for a 50 lb (22.60 kg) carp, in the same way that a budding match angler is unlikely to fish the 1st Division National in his first season.

Let us assume that some anglers form themselves into a specimen group with a view to catching big fish and they don't have access to any private syndicate waters. In their first year they will possibly be content if between them they catch a 2 lb (900 g) roach, a 6 lb (3 kg) tench or a double-figure pike. And yet, when you consider that in any one season an angler like Kevin Clifford might catch four or five tench over 6 lb (3 kg), a pike over 20 lb (9 kg), a carp over 20 lb (9 kg), three or four roach over 2 lb (900 g) and possibly two or three zander over 10 lb (4.50 kg) it gives some indication as to the difference between the angler starting in the world of specimen hunting and the men at the top. Skill is of course a crucial factor, but gaining access to waters that hold big fish is the key. You cannot catch 20 lb (9 kg) pike in waters that do not hold 20 lb (9 kg) pike. The secret, then, is to

The specimen hunter set up for a night's fishing. Note how everything is laid out to hand, an advantage when night falls.

fish the right waters.

Finding the right waters can be frustrating and time consuming. The easiest way is to buy an ordnance survey map of your own area and you will be surprised how many lakes and pits are shown that you did not know existed. Having pin-pointed each one, pay them a visit. Try to go at the weekend for the chances are that if anglers are fishing these waters, this is the time that they are likely to be there. Watching other anglers fish is often a good guide to what the water holds. If the anglers present are loose feeding maggots and whipping out small roach, this is not the type of water you are looking for. If, on the other hand, the anglers are fishing with two or even three rods and are seated on bed chairs, then in one respect you have struck gold for these are sure to be specimen hunters. What you have to ascertain now is who owns the fishing rights. If it is a club, you should be able to join. It may even be a free water, or it could be controlled by a private syndicate. If this is the case, it becomes difficult, because very few syndicate waters are open to the general public. Do not be put off if each time you find water, it is either full of small roach, or privately owned. The road to the top is never easy, which is why only the most dedicated anglers ever aspire to that exalted position.

That secrecy exists in specimen hunting is unquestionable: how often have you read, '30 lb carp from Northamptonshire lake' or, '10 lb bream from Cheshire mere', and cursed the writer for not being more specific? This situation must exist if big fish are to be caught consistently. Much time and effort go into the capture of a big fish; if anglers were to publicize these waters, they would quickly be overrun by enthusiastic amateurs, who would not necessarily spoil the fishery, but they would make the capture of further fish even more difficult. Hence the need for secrecy. If on your travels you found a water which held fish of record proportions, would you tell everybody about it? Of course not.

Since the 1950s, when Dick Walker caught his record carp, specimen hunting has become much more sophisticated. Tackle has improved out of all proportion and since the formation of the National Association of Specimen Groups in the mid-1960s, the whole specimen hunting community has benefited greatly from a tremendous pooling of information, especially within the specimen groups themselves. An angler wishing to take up specimen hunting can cut many corners by joining a local specimen group. Most groups consist of between four and ten members; some are larger, of course. Within the group all information is pooled; waters, baits and so on. Some groups lease their own water, others do not, but all have access to good waters.

Feeding

Unlike match anglers, who believe it is the way in which they feed fish that dictates what they catch, many specimen anglers tend to work on the premise that if they sit at the water's edge for long enough, eventually a big fish will pick up their bait. In some respects this is correct, but the specimen hunter is not averse to catching several big fish, so it follows that a well-presented carpet of groundbait will attract more fish into a swim than 56 lb (25.40 kg) of sweetcorn thrown indiscriminately over a lake.

Specimen fish are generally adult fish that have possibly been caught three or four times in their lives. They may have been caught many more times; we have no way of knowing, but what we do know is that they are far less impetuous than their younger brethren. Consequently, if we are going to catch big fish in any numbers, the 'chuck it and chance it' method is not the way. Having established that the water which we are about to fish holds a head of big fish, let us assume that the fish in question are bream. First of all, we must establish where the fish live. We know that at certain times of the year fish live in different parts of the lake. That isn't to say that they don't move around - of course they do - but the chances are that there is an area in the lake where they reside and feed for long periods, often in the evening or early morning.

It is an interesting fact that the shoal into which a fish is born is the shoal in which it will spend the rest of its life. This accounts for the fact that often, if you catch three fish in quick succession, they are invariably around the same size. This is the case particularly with bream. If you ever see a photograph of an angler with a number of bream of different sizes, for example, two of 4 lb (1.80 kg) and one of 6½ lb (3.40 kg), it is odds on that the larger fish was caught at a different time of the day and came from a different shoal. A shoal of bream might start out 100 strong, but as time goes on, predators, anglers and natural diseases will eventually dissipate the shoal to such an extent that a shoal of 8-9 lb (3.60-4 kg) bream may be as small as only six or seven fish. With this in mind scattering sweetcorn all over a 20 acre (8 hectare) mere or lake cannot make the job of catching these fish any easier.

What we need to do is to concentrate our groundbait into as small an area as possible, ensuring that the groundbait is liberally laced with hook samples. Bear in mind, that when a 8 lb (3.60 kg) bream moves on to your feed he can easily mop up a pint of maggots in no time at all, so make sure you have put enough feed to get the shoal feeding properly.

Much has been written on the advantages of using swimfeeders when fishing at distance, and while I agree with the theory that your hookbait is very close to the contents of the swimfeeder, I feel that a swimfeeder, to be really effective, must be fished over a bed of groundbait. It is impossible to cast a feeder 55 yd (50 m) accurately and by that I mean within a 13 ft (4 m) square. Consequently you finish up with little clumps of feed all over the lake. It

John Bailey returns a large barbel to the River Wensum.

John Watson with a 20-lb (9-kg) or over mirror carp: taken on luncheon meat at 66 yd (60 m).

makes more sense to lay down a carpet of groundbait, which can be fed accurately with a catapult, and then to fish the feeder over the top of it.

The groundbait will not only stop a passing shoal, it will also hold them. To my mind, using the swimfeeder on its own will only account for one fish as the shoal passes. There is not enough feed there to hold a shoal of six or seven 8 lb (3.60 kg) bream long enough for you to catch two or even three.

Speak to any specimen hunter and he will tell you that patience is a crucial factor in the pursuit of big fish and whilst I agree with that, I still feel that by sensible feeding it is often possible to put more than one fish on the bank.

Graham Marsden once wrote, 'Specimen hunting is a mixture of luck and skill, the skill is in getting the fish to pick up your bait and the luck comes in when there are two fish in your swim, a six pounder and a ten pounder, if the ten pounder picks up your bait, that's luck'. As in all forms of fishing, luck plays its part. This is demonstrated by the fact that of all the record fish, only one came as the result of a planned campaign, that being Dick Walker's 44 lb (20 kg) carp from Redmire. Dick knew of the existence of the fish and set about catching it. Having said that, he spent 460 hours fishing for it, and that was on a small water where there were a number of record-sized fish swimming around.

Graham Marsden has spent many years fishing a lake which he knows holds bream in excess of 15 lb (6.80 kg) yet he and his equally able fishing colleagues have yet to hook one of these fish, although fish in the 9 lb (4 kg) and 10 lb (4.50 kg) class have been caught. Possibly one day an angler will hook one. Will it be luck?

As specimen hunting has developed, so have baits, and nowhere is this more apparent than in the field of carp fishing. Many carp anglers tend to fish for carp to the exclusion of all other fish. They are among the largest coarse fish swimming in our waters and certainly the most intelligent. This is not so apparent in the young 3-4 lb (1.30-1.80 kg) class fish, but as carp grow

in size, they become increasingly more difficult to catch. Ashlea Pool, which is controlled by a private syndicate of top carp anglers, is an example of this. It is stocked with large carp, many of them over 20 lb (9 kg) and it has produced only three fish in a whole season yet this water is fished almost every weekend.

Because of the carp's ability to recognize anglers' baits, some carp anglers have gone to extremes in bait production, using amino acids and other chemical substances to catch their fish. In many cases, I feel that they have lost sight of what the sport is all about. In recent years we have seen the emergence of people who are known as the 'ultra cult' anglers. They are instant carp anglers; men who, because the most sophisticated tackle is now available to everybody, as are high-protein baits, do not graduate to big fish through the normal channels. These are the same people who seek publicity and give specimen hunting a bad name.

Tackle

In the 1950s when Dick Walker, Pete Frost, Peter Stone and Fred J. Taylor were proving to the angling world that the consistent capture of big fish was possible, there was little in the way of specialist tackle available through the normal fishing tackle shops. The original MK4 carp and Avon rods were both designed by Dick Walker and his friends, as were the Arlesey bomb and the electronic bite indicators.

Since that time, the development of specialist tackle has been tremendous, not only in the field of rods, but also of bite indication, nets, lines and hooks. The newcomer can now equip himself completely without having to design or modify his tackle. Fine anglers like Terry Eustace, Bruce Ashby, Allan Brown, and Trevor Moss are now able to make a living from manufacturing and selling specialist tackle, so great is the demand. Gone are the days when the specialist angler needed to have a lathe set up in his garden shed in order to make his own equipment. In fact, such is the standard set by men like Terry Eustace, that it is unlikely that the average angler could produce such fine

Previous page: *A superb example of a specimen tench.*

rods himself.

Fishing should be fun; the pursuit of a big fish should be enjoyable, not an obsession. The big fish scene has had its casualties, men who have had nervous breakdowns because they became obsessed with catching a single fish. Sport should never have this effect on people. Most of the top specimen anglers enjoy their fishing. They often fish at inconvenient hours, and through the night, not because they have secrets they don't want to share, but simply because that is the time when really big fish usually feed.

If you have the desire to become a successful specimen hunter, you must firstly become a successful angler and there is no quick route to consistent success. You might be lucky enough to find a water that holds big fish; given enough time you might catch one or two, but it is consistency that makes an angler into a good angler. Somebody once said that if the top specimen anglers had taken up match fishing they would have been just as successful and vice versa and that is a view I concur with totally. A good specimen angler is a good angler.

14
THE GREAT ANGLERS

When you consider that there are reputed to be four million anglers in the United Kingdom, it gives a real insight into how difficult it is to become a truly great angler. And the truth is, that only a handful of men qualify for that title. Anglers of the calibre of Ivan Marks, Kevin Ashurst, Dick Walker, Jack Hilton, Freddie Foster and Benny Ashurst are few and far between.

What separates these men from ordinary anglers is largely explainable but, as is so often the case with the truly great sportsmen, there is always that element of mystique. They have the ability to see a situation which others would miss; they enjoy the rare understanding of fish behaviour, without being able to explain why. They are also great innovators; was it not Freddie Foster who showed the real potential of the swingtip, and Dick Walker who conceived the Arlesey bomb, and Ivan Marks who designed the Pacemaker float and made groundbaiting at a distance of 66 yd (60 m) look easy?

With the exception of Freddie Foster and Jack Hilton, I have known the other anglers well and I have fished with Kevin and Ivan many times. For the most part, they look to be simply good anglers; like Bobby Charlton in football and Clive Lloyd in cricket, they do not show their real genius all of the time; in fact I have seen both Kevin and Ivan look very ordinary, but put them under pressure and suddenly they begin to be in a class of their own.

Most anglers start fishing as boys, often being taught by friends or relations with a limited knowledge of the sport, and the bad habits of the teacher are passed on to the pupil. Both Ivan and Kevin benefited from great teachers, in Benny Ashurst and Eddie Allan. This, of course, must be a contributary factor to their success; however, it would be a fool who suggests that this was the sole reason. Two things each of these anglers enjoys, are an undying love of angling and a remarkable memory for angling incidents. The number of times I have fished matches with Ivan Marks and while walking to our pegs he has recalled that such and such a chap won a match on that peg with 20 lb (9 kg) in 1975, or so-and-so won there with 12 lb (5.40 kg) in 1974, and yet the same fellow has been to my home fifty times and still has difficulty finding it.

I do not believe that an angler can make himself into a great angler. Many anglers, given time and dedication can become top specimen hunters or match anglers, but to achieve greatness I believe that an angler has to be born with that special understanding of the sport. I once saw Kevin win a match having fed nothing for three hours; all around him anglers were showering in maggots and groundbait and catching just the odd small fish while Kevin caught skimmer bream. After the match I asked him why, after two hours, he had stopped feeding? In that well-rounded Lancashire accent he said, 'They didn't want it Dave'. That is the indescribable quality; nobody else in that match recognized that situation, although there were a number of good anglers fishing.

Dick Walker is an enigma, a university graduate, in fact an intellectual in what is looked upon as a working-class sport. His contribution to specimen hunting in the 1950s and 1960s is incalculable; he revolutionized tackle design and he wrote about and caught a 40 lb (18.10 kg) carp when a fish of half that size was looked upon as a massive fish. He wrote that the National Championship would be won by an angler legering, when the method was in its infancy. Even today he continues to be a major force through his books and weekly column in the *Angling Times.* In recent years he has devoted more of his time to reservoir fly fishing, designing rods, creating new flies and catching big trout. In fact, until it was beaten by Alan Pearson's fish, Dick Walker held the rainbow trout record with a fish of 18 lb 4 oz (8.20 kg) from Sam Holland's Abingdon pool.

Unlike other sports, such as football, cricket, darts, and golf, anglers are confronted with a different set of circumstances each time they go fishing. Can you imagine how difficult golf would become if nobody knew where the holes were? I wonder how many below par golfers we would have were this the case. Imagine how difficult darts would become if the board was moved after every throw? It is this ability to understand fish movement and habits instinctively that sets the great anglers apart from the rest, they seem to enjoy a sixth sense. Benny Ashurst, who is over sixty years old, still goes fishing every day, and still has an almost childlike love of the sport. He wins over £1000 every year and how many anglers can claim that distinction. In fact, Benny is so good that years ago, before the open match circuit was really established, he was banned from many local matches simply because it was a foregone conclusion that he would win. I recall Roy Marlow once telling me that when he first

Blackpool pike angler, John Watson, returns a 24 lb 8 oz (11-kg) Lomond pike.

Two of England's most successful match men, Ken Giles (rear) and Clive Smith.

met Ivan Marks, Ivan was only allowed to fish for three hours of a five-hour match. One year the club with which they both fished ran nineteen matches; Ivan fished for his allotted three hours and won every one. What is more, at that time he was only in his teens.

The beauty of angling is that it can be enjoyed at all levels; the man who dangles a worm for a couple of hours on a Sunday morning can derive as much pleasure as the top matchmen. Because the sport offers little in the way of real financial gain, very few people take up the sport in order to further their careers. Kevin, Benny, Ivan and Dick have achieved greatness, but not as a result of a well-planned career or a shrewd business manager, merely as a result of pursuing the sport that they love. They enjoy a rare quality which sets them apart from the rest of us, and have made great contributions to the sport.

IN CONCLUSION

It has always been my opinion that, as anglers, we have a responsibility to leave the fishing for future generations, if not better, then at least as good as we found it. We live in an industrial age; pollution is a constant problem and the angling administrators must fight to preserve our fisheries. The ACA, the NASG and the NFA are all voluntary associations that need your support. And do not leave discarded line and litter on the banksides, it is both dangerous and unsightly. We must protect our environment; it is not a pleasure to fish on a lake that resembles a rubbish tip.

Angling is a great sport which brings out the best in people. Let us protect it.

Anglers at their pegs in a match on the Grand Union Canal.

GLOSSARY

antenna a type of waggler

Arlesey bomb a pear-shaped leger weight with a swivel inserted in the top, designed by Richard Walker.

back shot a small shot placed 12 in (30 cm) above the float to assist in sinking the line.

bale arm the metal arm which picks up the reel line and wraps it around the spool.

balsa a type of soft wood used in the construction of floats.

bait anything used to catch fish.

bait dropper a spring-loaded cylinder used to drop bait on the river bed.

barbel a fleshy appendage found near the mouth of barbel and carp.

bite alarm battery-controlled buzzer, used by specimen hunters as a bite indicator.

blank an expression used by anglers to describe a fishless session; also a hollow fibreglass tube from which rods are made.

blockend feeder a swimfeeder which has both ends sealed.

bloodworm tiny red worm used in conjunction with Jokers. A continental technique now used by many British anglers, especially on the north-west canals.

blued hook a type of small fine wire hook, often used in conjunction with bloodworm.

bread flake small pieces of fresh bread, pinched on to the hook.

bread punch a small cutting tube which punches out small pellets of bread, for use as hookbait.

breaking strain the manufacturers' estimate of the amount of strain the line will take before it breaks. This is generally gauged when the line is dry, the 'wet strength' of many lines can be as much as 20 per cent less than that stated on the spool.

bristle very fine tip found on pole floats.

bronze maggots of the many different colours that maggots have been dyed, bronze maggots accounted for more fish during the 1970s than any other colour.

bubble float a round plastic float, into which water can be put, which gives weight for casting. It is used mainly by pike anglers.

butt indicator a bite indicator.

caster the chrysalis of the maggot.

centre pin reel a revolving drum type of reel, used mainly on fast-flowing rivers.

clutch adjustable rachet which allows a surging fish to pull line off a reel.

coffin lead coffin-shaped leger weight.

cork often used to form the body of a waggler.

creel angler's wicker basket.

dead bait dead fish used as bait for pike, zander and eels.

disgorger device for removing hook from fish's throat.

dorsal fin fin found on top of a fish's body.

dough-bobbin indicator placed on the line between the reel and the buff ring; movement of the line causes the indicator to rise or fall off the line, indicating a bite.

elastic used in conjunction with the continental pole.

elver a small eel.

float a bite indicator usually made of wood, reed or bird quill.

foul hooked a fish hooked in the fin or the body.

freeline a method of fishing, requiring neither float or leger; the bait is cast into a river and allowed to swing freely in the current.

fry young fish.

gaff a metal hook fixed to a shaft, used mainly by salmon anglers for lifting fish from the water.

gorge baiting an illegal method of fishing for pike; it allows the fish to eat the bait, taking the hooks down to its stomach, and resulting in a dead pike.

gozzer fresh home-bred maggot.

ground bait fresh crumb, used as a carrier to get bait to fish which are not close enough to accept loose feed.

holdall a rod carrier.

hook length length of nylon to which the hook is tied. This is always of less breaking strain than the line. In the event of the hook being snagged, the line breaks below the float, so that expensive floats are not lost.

keep net a cylindrical net sealed at one end, used by fishermen for retaining fish.

lead various forms of weights used for sinking the line and holding the bait in position.

legering a method of fishing a stationary bait.

line bite a false bite, caused by a fish swimming into the line, making the indicator move.

loaded float a float with weight loaded into the base.

maggot the larva of the fly used as bait.

marker a mark used to cast to, when legering.

match a competition where anglers draw pegs, and the angler who catches the biggest weight of fish wins.

micro shot very small lead shot.

mouse droppings cylindrical shot, used when fishing with hemp on the hook.

mystic bait substitute of French origin.

paste a hookbait made by soaking bread in water, the water is squeezed out and the bread kneeded into a paste.

paternoster a means of attaching an Arlesey bomb to the line, for legering.

peg a numbered position in a match.

pinkie a small pink-tinged maggot.

plug an artificial pike bait, made of wood or plastic.

plummet a lead weight used in ascertaining the depth of water.

pole a fibreglass or carbon pole used for fishing.

quill the centre shaft of a bird feather used to make floats.

quivertip a fine piece of glass fibre which is screwed into the tip section of a leger rod, acting as a bite indicator.

ratchet a checking device on a reel to prevent line running out freely.

rod rest a piece of forked metal which supports the rod.

rod rings guides whipped on to a rod, which allow the free passage of line and spread the load of the fish along the whole length of the rod.

sliding float a float used for fishing water in excess of 12 ft (3.60 m) deep. The float is fished loose with a stop knot holding it in position at the correct depth.

snap tackle two treble hooks on a wire trace on to which a live or dead fish is mounted, for pike fishing.

specimen fish a large fish of any species.

spigot a method for joining the sections of a fishing rod together.

spoon and spinners artificial lures used for pike fishing.

spring quivertip a form of quivertip with a length of spring inserted close to the base.

stop knot a knot which is tied on to the line which can be moved, this knot is used in conjunction with a sliding float.

strike a sharp upward movement of the rod, that sets the hook in the mouth of a biting fish.

swimfeeder a plastic container fixed to the line and filled with bait. Once on the river bed the bait escapes through the holes which are drilled in the sides of the container.

swingtip a swinging arm, through which line is fed; when a biting fish takes the bait the tip, which is screwed into the rod, is lifted.

swivel a metal device for joining lines together; it also prevents line twist.

tares a type of pea, fished in conjunction with hemp; this can be a devastating roach bait in the summer.

terminal tackle an expression used for describing the line and shot set up, below the float, i.e. that which is in the water.

wasp grub the contents of a wasp nest, used as a fishing bait.

wire trace multi-strand wire used to form the terminal rig for pike fishing.

worms a fishing bait.

Two specimen hunters bream fishing on the Norfolk Broads.

INDEX